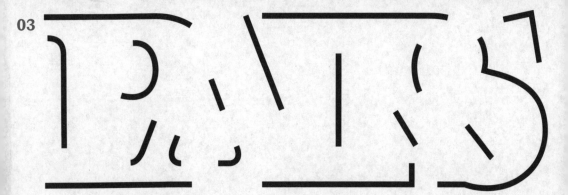

Edited by Olivia Howard,
Adrea Piazza, and Kyle Winston

Distributed by Harvard University Press
London, England, and Cambridge, Massachusetts

A couple of years ago, in 2020, *Pairs* arrived amid the pandemic and faced the challenge of bridging isolation with dialogue at a time when "suddenly, people and objects couldn't be brought together."[①] However, for *Pairs* 03, the journal has returned to the school for the first time. So, how fitting that this return to physical proximity should also mark the 50th anniversary of George Gund Hall, the home of the Harvard Graduate School of Design. The place where we all gather and work in the five-story open air "trays," where models and drawings accrue on desks, living the vision of Gund's architect John Andrews that the building "give[s] the opportunity for people to get together," as he mused in a 1979 short film on his work. He specified: "A student, for instance, may fly a paper airplane, and when retrieving that paper airplane, might meet a landscape architect. Or an urban designer, hearing a radio somewhere and wanting to turn it off, may get into a little bit of a fight. But still by the same token it provides that little bit of visual and mental communication."[②]

3

For *Pairs* 03, we conducted interviews in person for the first time. We walked along Le Corbusier's Carpenter Center ramp to discuss collaboration and revision, and we visited the greenhouses at Harvard's Arnold Arboretum to explore the reinvention of plant species outside of their natural environments. One contributor traveled from Cambridge all the way to Venice to speak with filmmakers about a documentary that followed the construction of Gund Hall. Meanwhile, an editor hopped on a train to New York to talk to a writer about a 1930s newsreel and all the unseen labor that builds the world we live in.

We finally got to do what the journal intended. So, what is the result? We realized that the pairs in *Pairs* are more than just an attempt at making a connection. Instead, like Andrews's building, they entail layering relationships—planned and unplanned, antagonistic and friendly—so that connection is not forced through isolation but comes from the joy of simply being together (conversation being the pleasant inevitability).

This idea extended to this issue's graphic design so that the physical object of the journal reflects the themes of superimposition and the simultaneity explored in many of our conversations. For example, we resurfaced memories of Harvard's campus in a conversation with a poet about a room dedicated to the recorded history of the art form and a landscape historian peeled away the layers of the envelopes and taxonomies that contain a butterfly collection. When an interview recording was lost to the digital ether, we recovered its content through a second dialogue, deepening the conversation rather than abridging it. One artist considered flowers that never fade. And, over coffee, another artist, whose work explores the reaches of fiction, shared her ambivalence about nostalgia while discussing dream spaces.

Despite this being our third issue, we are still a journal of firsts—*prima voltita!*—and we'd like to keep it that way. The intent is to create new encounters and an element of surprise, which is essential to the journal's subject–object pairing. However, some firsts were disappointing. Early in the production of this issue, we were stood up for an interview. The bouquet the contributor brought along as a thank you wilted in our office. Meanwhile, an older interview—one we loved but had to set aside—came back into play. So, in case you are feeling nostalgic for those chance encounters and serendipitous connections that were seemingly on pause while we were all away, please know that happy accidents are alive and well—along with a healthy dose of misadventure— and reside here in the pages of *Pairs* 03.

Olivia, Adrea, and Kyle

5

① Nicolás Delgado Alcega, Vladimir Gintoff, and Kimberley Huggins, foreword to *Pairs* 01 (Spring 2021).
② *Architecture - A Performing Art*, directed by Michael Robertson (1979; Pyrmont: National Film and Sound Archive; Film Australia Collection), 10:12–10:34.

Ila Bêka and Louise Lemoine ⟶ are filmmakers, educators, and publishers exploring contemporary urbanism through lived experience, trading conventional architectural representations for deeply personal visual descriptions. They currently teach in the Diploma Programme at the Architectural Association in London and gave their first public lecture at the GSD in 2013.

Building Gund Hall ⟶ is a 16mm film chronicling the construction of the new home for the GSD from October 1969 to August 1972. Designed by Australian architect John Andews, 2022 marks the building's 50th anniversary. The film, directed by Len Gittleman, is part documentary, part art film, part drama, with shots alternating between comedic (and at times poetic) time lapses with messy on-the-ground close-ups of tradesmen screwing, nailing, and jamming parts together

Bêka
ouise
oine
ding Hall

Julia Spackman

JULIA SPACKMAN

Have you both visited Gund Hall before?

LOUISE LEMOINE

Yes, we actually gave the first lecture of our lives there. Our first film, *Koolhaas House Life*, was screened at Gund after an interested student invited us.

JS

We'll have to invite you back! How did the film *Building Gund Hall* relate to your memory of the building? Did you approach the project differently?

LL

The first crucial question that will determine the kind of film you will make has to do with understanding the moment in the building's life that you're going to portray. Is it following the conception? During the process of construction? The Gund Hall film gives particular focus to the process, the elaboration, the effort, and the labor. Also, sometimes in the film, some doubts or small issues arise. *Building Gund Hall* dives into the vivid questions and complexities of making architecture.

JS

The film presents the building's construction as a grand choreography of labor but also as a point of contention among the parties involved. Superimposed titles like "Architect" and "Roofer" emphasize this division. It's most extreme when all the trade and client representatives are present at tests for the fiberglass truss covers. People only are given identifiers when they—

LL

—represent their role—

The first tree felled at the Gund Hall site, at the corner of Cambridge and Quincy streets, October 1969. *Building Gund Hall*, 1972, video still, 00:47.
Model by John Andrews Architects for Gund Hall presented at the groundbreaking ceremony, November 1969. *Building Gund Hall*, 1972, video still, 01:4

Meeting to determine final details of the roof and installation of fiberglass truss enclosures, April 29, 1971. *Building Gund Hall*, 1972, video stills, 06:46; 10:11.

JS

—and engage with doubt. The film dramatizes construction, moving between documentation and narrative. These scenes substantiate some of the conflicts of that time.

LL

But I think a project always entails moments of tension among different parties. The film uncovers different views of the same project, different points of entry and expectations, or different projected intentions. Reducing the person to their role lets us understand those perspectives, casting the parties almost like chess pieces in the sense that certain actors represent certain actions.

9

JS

But the film doesn't totally abstract the actors—I mean, workers. It romanticizes labor in close shots of hands torquing and banging. In one moment, a painter engages with the camera by writing an advertisement on the elevator lobby wall. There are only a couple of moments like this.

LL

It evokes a particular temporality for the project. I think the film's ambition was to underline the work, labor, attention, complexity, detail, etc., that go into a building's elaboration more so than to sacralize the finalized design.

JS

Construction is absolutely more triumphant than a post-occupancy narrative of the building. Filming it now would show the scattered trash cans used to collect roof water when it rained. There's quite a lot of glass.

LL

In the summer, is it super hot?

ILA BÊKA

Super, super hot.

LL

It's a little bit like a greenhouse.

JS

It is, exactly. It even faces east.

LL

So, you're growing inside.

IB

The students are the plants!

JS

Just thinking about it feels dehydrating.

LL

Start as a seed, and then you grow into a flower.

One day of sun, as seen from William James Hall. *Building Gund Hall*, 1972, video stills, 17:20–17:30.

IB

Like a jungle.

JS

We're a crowded plot now.

LL

It's interesting when a school's identity is so bound to a building. For example, the Architectural Association in London needs more buildings, but the identity of the school is linked to the building on Bedford Square. How do you keep the school's spirit while engaging with expansion and renewal? That's complex.

JS

Can you say more about methods or intentions you might have to communicate in relation to the sensory experience of being in a place?

LL

This is a central topic for us. We make films that function similarly to the ways in which our emotional memory regards spatial exploration. Our memory works as a filter, and it's very selective because otherwise we would be nuts. After visiting a space, your memory will not rebuild that experience in a chronological, rational, or progressive way, but you will be able to remember what impacted you the most emotionally through moments of intensity and feeling. This is partly an unconscious process.

JS

Is that disorienting? Many of your viewers have architecture backgrounds and might expect the films to deliver a complete spatial understanding, bit by bit. Do you use montage to subvert this norm?

LL

Architectural photography often aims for visual efficiency—in one image, you need to understand everything. Our films deconstruct the unity of assembled architectural elements and through confusion allow entry with your emotions rather than with your rational spatial understanding.

11

IB

It may be disorienting only in that we avoid being didactic as we trust our spectators to make their way through. We don't like films that explicitly say what you should see and understand. Structurally, we build our films through a series of fragments that relate to the moments of intensity within a specific place.

LL

We work with disorientation and fragmentation in a very playful way. Like a game, the spectator builds their understanding of the whole film with little pieces. It's a mental exercise.

IB

We give you the elements, and you build it up. So, interpretations are flexible and depend on the viewer.

LL

We actively address the spectator's curiosity. We reject narrative strategies of explanation, such as voice-overs, that assume the spectator will be half absent in the act of watching.

IB

In our case, we ask for full attention.

LL

Watching film is not a passive act but rather all about intentionally confronting a work. The same is true for other types of artworks, be it painting, literature, etc.

IB

From the very beginning, we emphasized the language of the body in order to make films that communicate our physical perception of space. In cinema, the first thing that you have to decide is where to put the camera. Instead of letting the film be led by technical issues, we think first about where to place our body in space. The camera placement shows how we relate ourselves to the space and to others. For example, our film series *Homo Urbanus* was all shot

Assembled truss levitating at the factory. *Building Gund Hall*, 1972, video stills, 13:36; 13:38.

in the street with a wide-angle lens that required us to be very close to people, and thus we were very physically engaged in the process. We use cinematographic techniques in working with our students to recount the sensorial experience of presence, perception, and spatial situation.

LL

We don't stage things. What's happening in our films is not composed for the frame of the camera. Most architectural films present a staged reality that seeks out the maximum aesthetic effect and is the product of total directorial control. We intend to disrupt those rules. If we shoot in bad weather conditions, for instance, this is not a minor detail but an intentional provocation underlining the fact that we work with reality as it is, with all its unforeseen events.

JS

How does editing play into this? If filming realistically portrays lived events, then does editing create the memory of the moment?

IB

What fascinates me is that memory is closely linked to the structure of language. We know, scientifically, that memories are fragmented when stored in our brains. When we recall a memory it undergoes a process of reordering.

LL

Which also imposes a chronology.

IB

Your mind is restructuring everything. Your brain will collect parts of a memory from here and there and recompose them. There's a mess inside your brain. But when I talk, I follow a process of rationalization. There's a certain similarity between spoken language and film editing. It's a similar process of recomposing order and chronology from fragmented elements. Our editing process attempts to escape this excess logic imposed by language.

LL

We do not write scripts in the classical sense but instead use a graphic constellation of topics linked by dynamic association. Ila is very involved in music, and we try to edit the films following the principle of harmony of musical composition, which allows us to work more intuitively.

13

IB

Language communication is very efficient because rules provide clarity—or at least it should be most of the time, even though I may not sound so clear now! You come from the United States to interview us, and we are in front of you bombarding you with words and crazy ideas that probably don't make much sense. When you get back to school, you might say, "I didn't understand anything because they talked about making music, I don't know how to compose this interview. Beautiful sounds, but nonsense."

JS

I have some ideas for how to edit this together!

IB

It can sound a bit absurd, but that's how we work on film editing.

LL

The way architecture uses film is very often in the vein of a well-executed and nicely shot promotional spot. The film is efficient, clear, and easy. That's why we had to be quite brutal at the start to

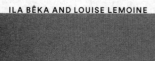

break with those expectations. We invite our spectator to appreciate our films through experiential and emotional discovery.

JS

The absence in narration feels natural after a while, which makes any return of the human subject surprising. There's a moment in *Barbicania* where the model comes down the stairs and confronts the camera.[①] This felt serendipitous or, like you said, unplanned. Are there days when you can go on site and not film anything at all? Days when nothing strikes you?

IB

We said earlier that we avoid script writing, and that's true. Instead, we work very much on maintaining an active state of openness and curiosity. If you are open-minded, something will necessarily happen. It's up to you to catch that thing. The quality of observation depends essentially on your state of sensitivity, receptivity, and listening. This is the central question we also work on with students.

LL

Very strangely, observation is not a skill architecture schools train students in, and it's largely neglected, I would say. Architects carry the responsibility of shaping the spaces in which we will live, so their actions are very impactful. How can architects correctly answer to real needs without first observing and listening carefully?

IB

Students spend five or more years enclosed within the walls of a school where teachers explain the making of things. When the students finally get out, they hardly know anything about the outside world: humanity, society, and how social and cultural dynamics are embedded in space. Walking in the street they hardly notice anything around them because they haven't been trained.

① *Barbicania*, directed by Bêka & Lemoine (2014, Bêka & Partners with the support of Barbican Center and Fluxus Projects), 1 hr., 30 min. HD, color with sound.

The great missing character is the individual. Spaces are most of the time represented as empty or with only silhouettes.

…ne day of sun, as seen from William James Hall. *Building Gund Hall*, 1972, video stills, 17:20–17:30.

LL

An architectural photographer will often put people aside to take his photographs, transforming architecture as an abstract object of design.

IB

Architecture is a discipline, I think, that requires generosity and altruism. That's how we understand the role of observation in architecture. You will reach a good design if you first try to understand something about humanity. I don't remember anyone talking about this when I was studying architecture in Venice. No one. One of my teachers was Aldo Rossi, and at the end of the year, you could see that all the student projects were copies of Aldo Rossi.

LL

With the little flag of Aldo Rossi?

15

IB

With the flag. It was the same. We were clones, no? We were making the same things as the teacher.

JS

But isn't that type of learning productive? Once learned, an academic design personality is easily taken off. I think there's value in trying on a professor's thinking, at least temporarily.

LL

A school should help the students to become themselves, not just please the professors. That's my view.

IB

I can understand what you've said about studying with different teachers. And at the end you choose a mix for yourself. But instead of this, can you imagine a kind of teaching that fosters uncertainty? After each session, you'll be more confused, and confused, and confused. And through confusion, you will be pushed to define yourself and better understand what you want to do.

LL

That's why at the AA, we've developed a process that is close to psychoanalysis in the sense that we are not here to give you answers or truth but to support the birth of your most personal ideas.

IB

Architecture education rarely gives value to intuition or to getting lost. These are mostly considered dangerous.

Workers fixing translucent fiberglass shell in place over white truss. *Building Gund Hall*, 1972, video still, 19:36.

LL

We think it is a necessary step for our students to get lost, or at least feel like they're getting lost. If you don't get lost, this is a bit worrying for us. Getting lost is when you start to think by yourself, independent of others' processes and road maps.

JS

You might then be encouraged by a couple things happening at the GSD currently. I feel very lost right now in my studio: I have no program, no site, just a collection of visual intentions.

LL

Be happy with this.

JS

I'm content but also nervous. This conversation has calmed those thoughts, though. I know this disconcerting open-mindedness is planned.

IB

To get lost has to be a part of a program. Not in the sense of missing information, but as a mental process. This is different.

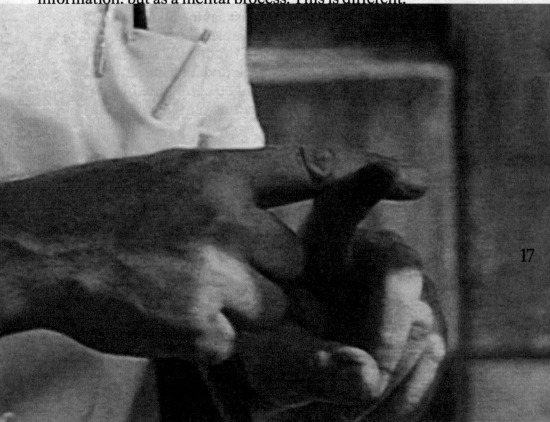

17

chitect on-site at fiberglass installation gesturing. *Building Gund Hall*, 1972, video still, 18:49.

JS

So that your mind is open to making new connections.

LL

If you want to build your way, you need to deconstruct the falsehood that everything is clearly rational. You need to initiate your journey. This implies a lot of uncertainty, so be confident.

JS

How do you prop your mind open against forces insistent on its closing?

IB

Focus on seeing. You can see in front of you, but you can also see from inside of you. A very simple exercise we often do with students is to look at a white wall for an hour. First it seems absurd. You don't get the sense of it. Then slowly you will discover that this white wall has an incredible amount of information that you couldn't see at first. It's a matter of time but also attention and the scale of looking.

LL

I think this really relates to what we were just saying about having confidence in your intuition and being available. The pressure of efficiency is a problem for the student, of finding the super idea in five minutes. Be more gentle with yourself and for a longer time, don't oppress your mind with the results. If you enter into this state of availability and open yourself to the surrounding stimuli, something will arise.

IB

If you are available and curious, you will discover incredible stories. We are all reservoirs of incredible stories. We haven't talked about you, but I'm sure you have many stories to tell.

JS

Thank you for sharing yours.

LL

Enjoy it here. These are the very first days of autumn.

IB

Get lost in Venice!

Spring clouds on Cambridge Street facade. *Building Gund Hall, 1972*, video stills, 27:36–27:47.

Kevin & Aalto's Woodberry Poetry Room

Kevin Young is the Andrew W. Mellon Director of the Smithsonian's National Museum of African American History and Culture and the *New Yorker*'s poetry editor. While a student at Harvard University, he was a member of the Dark Room Collective, a community of African American writers. Young is the author of fifteen books of poetry and prose and the editor of nine volumes of poetry.

Aalto's Woodberry Poetry Room is a special collections room designed in 1949 by Finnish architect Alvar Aalto and housed within Lamont Library in Harvard Yard. The Poetry Room is home to an unparalleled collection of 20th and 21st century English-language poetry books and serials, audio recordings, and rare materials. It reopened in 2006 following a contested renovation.

Young Mo's Poetry Room

> Emily Hsee

EMILY HSEE
What do you think the relationship is between poetry and built space?

KEVIN YOUNG
Both poetry and architecture are interested in structure. Somewhere in there, in the mix of structures, is what I'm searching for in my writing. And it's when I started understanding structure in poems that I think I became an actual poet who wrote the poems that became my first book.

I wrote most of that first book when I was at Harvard as an undergraduate, and most of it—three of the four sections—was about Louisiana, where my family's from and what we called "home" growing up. The rest of the book was about place and displacement— or maybe that was the whole book! So, if we consider space in the broadest way possible, I think about it a lot in my poetry.

"Home" is such a big word, but of course, space and architecture are associated with it. The houses I grew up in included many different kinds of architecture: ranch houses and split-levels and the kind of 1970s design one might come to know and love. But before that, the primary examples in my sense of space were the houses my parents were born in, which were still standing when I was little. We stayed in the house that my mom grew up in when we went to Louisiana until they built another house next door. My grandparents' houses are both these kind of two-sided shotgun houses that I associate with Louisiana, and of course, they're built on stilts like most houses there because of the water table.

The other sense of architecture I have is from driving by what used to be the house my paternal grandmother grew up in. They had stairs on the outside from the lower level to the upper level, and I remember vividly that feeling of Southern life. This—among other aspects of that life—was something I was really trying to capture in my poetry, but it was also something I think I instinctively but not consciously knew was disappearing. Surely no one's crying for outside stairs or an outhouse again. But in my recent book *Stones* the first poem is a poem of origins, of being from a place that's decidedly not like Harvard, let's say. The last line—"up from the dark / dank bottom springs a tree"—is about an outhouse and how from the essence, the horror of the body, and the things we leave behind comes the future.

EH
That's a beautiful way to put it. Do you think architecture, specifically modernist architecture, can or should invoke emotion in a way that poetry or music or fine arts do?

KY

I'm probably the wrong person to ask because I'm literally sitting in the National Museum of African American History and Culture, staring out at the Washington Monument in my office. I mean, you can maybe even see it—there you go. Can you see that?

EH

Wow, yes!

KY

The angle of the panels that encase the museum is the exact angle of the Washington Monument. When I found that out—how can you not be emotional about that? To me, this is a building that almost redefines the connection between modernism and emotion. But I also reject the notion that modernism and, say, African American culture are opposites. In fact, I would say that African American culture is at the heart of modernism. The desire for that kind of space owes something to African sculpture, African movement, and African American architectures and improvisations.

I also think we have to be specific about what kind of modernism we are talking about. When I was a student, I worked at Le Corbusier's Carpenter Center as a security guard. I would lock up and walk around the entire building, and I never thought of the building as abstract or emotional or cold or all the kinds of things people might suppose. Instead, to me, it was weird locks and windows and cool little spaces, and people working on art. I would see someone painting and say, "Hey, are you still working?" and they would say, "Yes," and I'd say, "Okay," and let them go on their way and continue locking up around them. It was a place of industry and art and reinvention. The other guards I knew who sat behind the desk were all in the Dark Room Collective.[①] So, I did not have the same feeling about modernist buildings. If anything, working there felt like a moment to reclaim or just lay claim to what was already ours and already there.

23

EH

I specifically remember walking up the stairs in the Carpenter Center and seeing a door with the strangest dimensions. I'm struggling to remember now if it was the narrowest or widest door I'd ever seen.

① Founded in Boston in 1988, the Dark Room Collective formed a community of Black writers and artists and a reading series celebrating emerging and established Black literature.

KY

Some of the doors are incredibly narrow. And I remember going through them and having to lock and check them.

The building is so different, and the siting is perfect but strange, almost like a spaceship landed in the middle of Harvard between the Fogg Museum and Lamont Library, with the Henry Moore sculpture across the street. It all seemed very dynamic, but it was also part of the landscape. The modernism I admire tried for that. Now, that doesn't mean it didn't sometimes want to be an incursion into the atmosphere and have you notice it, but that can take many forms.

The Woodberry Poetry Room was designed by Alvar Aalto in 1949. Houghton Library Repository at Harvard, ca. 1960s–1980s.

EH

Let's dive into the Woodberry Poetry Room at Lamont Library. You were at Harvard before the controversial 2006 renovation. In an email to me you said that you "haven't seen the new room and stubbornly don't want to." Could I ask why you're not interested in seeing it?

KY

I mean, I just haven't been back to see it, so there's nothing I can say about the renovation, I'm afraid.

EH

Right. So you're not necessarily opposed to the renovation itself?

KY

I can only tell you about what it meant to me way back when.

EH

Let's talk about the Woodberry Poetry Room you knew. What were your thoughts on the room when you were a student? What was your relationship to it?

KY

I wish I could remember when I discovered it. I spent a decent

iterary magazines line the entrance of the Woodberry Poetry Room. Houghton Library Repository at Harvard, ca. 1960s–1980s.

amount of time in Lamont, and for my mother who might read this, when my roommates said I was at the library, that was true! I must have discovered it my freshman year, because I began taking poetry classes then. I don't know what it's like now, but at that time you walked in and on the right was a bank of magazines facing out. Those literary magazines were really a lifeline for me. I would just read them and see what people were writing (and publishing). It was the only way you could discover new poems unless you went to a great bookstore. But there was something about this space and spending an afternoon perusing literary magazines for free and just for you. They had a really good selection, and from there I would figure out where I might send poems or where the poets I loved were appearing.

All around the room were bookcases. You could see the books on some, but others were just flat panels. They were so flat that it was only later in my Harvard existence that I saw someone open one of those panels. It was like magic. They looked like walls. Like, "What? Those have books in them?" Probably the semivaluable or rarer books lived there. I would just sit in the room or walk around the shelves and browse. It was what I think of as the perfect calm, quiet. And it had great comfortable chairs and stools, which I only later understood were by Alvar Aalto.

If there was someone at the desk, eight times out of 10 I knew who they were from the literary scene—it was a good job. So, it was a friendly, open place. And there were these glass-topped cabinets that were, I don't know, three-by-three square with rounded edges. I think it was only much, much later when I realized those were phonographs. You popped them up and you could play records on them.

Relatedly, I also did not know until later what an amazing reading series they had hosted over the years. They had all these important recordings from over the decades, which are now available online. I was reading people like John Berryman, who I didn't really like that much at the time, but later came to admire despite his flaws. And knowing that he had recorded there and read *The Dream Songs* meant a lot to me.[2]

It was a place I could write. It was a place where I did write some of what became my first book. It was very much a creative center, almost like a hive that I could climb into. It was a bit of a retreat, even from the rest of Lamont, which I also spent time in. The library had a really different feeling, but the poetry room was like its warm hearth. Now I know they had weird little corners in the back that held recordings and that you would only know about them if you were wise enough to request records for those lovely record players. But there was a kind of wonder even in that; it held potential, if that makes sense.

EH

Yes. I was reading about the history of the poetry room and the many ways in which it was revolutionary. My understanding is that it created a new social life around poetry and even being in a library. It introduced this idea that poetry, by nature of taking multiple forms, was this more dynamic and living thing, something to be seen

[2] John Berryman wrote *77 Dream Songs* in 1964. In 1965, it was awarded the Pulitzer Prize for Poetry.

and heard and felt. Even without knowing the more aural aspects of the Woodberry Poetry Room, do you think the design or the layout of the space contributed to that feeling?

KY

Yes, I mean, I love the space. It's hard to come by a space that always feels comfortable, that doesn't feel empty if you're there by yourself yet doesn't feel distracting if other people are present. It had this community quality, and like you were saying, it was a kind of hub. People went there if they were applying for magazines or submitting things; it was a drop-off spot, so it had a utility as well. It wasn't just this dreamy space. It helped that it also just a great name. "Wood," "berry"— and here you were in this wood-filled room.

EH

People often allude to the domestic quality of the space and how the idea of pleasure and comfort were important to the room's design, which was a new idea in relation to poetry, at least at Harvard. This "elite art form" could be experienced comfortably and pleasurably. You could feel like you were at home. As you put it, the warm hearth. Even the new audio technology was kind of disguised in this wooden box to almost make it seem like a piece of furniture. There was this softening and humanizing of the machine and accessibility to the inaccessible.

27

KY

I know Aalto wasn't American, but there was a kind of domestic Americanness. There was a feeling to it that was homey and localized, in a good way.

It was warm. It had that quality both from the wood and from the sort of experiences you had in there. And certainly if it were a techno library it wouldn't have had the same feeling, even if it had the same stuff in it. Sometimes poetry rooms can feel like precious rooms no one uses, but Woodberry didn't feel like that. It was a pleasurable place: I had many conversations about the latest gossip and the poetry world. There or was involved in starting two magazines, at least, maybe three. It was often the place for those kinds of crossroads.

EH

Do you think the room had a larger role in the poetry world in rethinking accessibility to or associations with poetry? Or was this just a Harvard space? It has a reputation for being this revolutionary space for making audio-poetry more accessible, but does that take away from the culture of spoken poetry or spoken word, which already had a rich history of being in the public realm?

Listening consoles housed in wood cases designed by Alvar Aalto. Houghton Library Repository at Harvard, ca. 1960s–1980s.

KY

The history of spoken-word poetry goes well beyond Harvard, obviously. I would argue the Harlem Renaissance has a lot to do with it. But when I was in Cambridge there was also a burgeoning open mic and slam scene, which we participated in, at least with the Dark Room. Open mics were mostly in other parts of Cambridge, Central Square, and Boston. I think these spaces are connected, though, and it wasn't either-or.

I don't want to overstate the Woodberry Poetry Room's presence. But I do think it's important to say that there were a plethora of poets at Harvard, and in Boston and Cambridge then, and you could meet many of them. You could hang out with Seamus Heaney (who I eventually studied with) or end up at a dinner with Derek Walcott and Seamus, or you could go see Joseph Brodsky read in Sanders Theatre alongside other soon-to-be Nobel laureates. It felt like poetry was part of campus life. I saw these giant poetry readings, but you could also see a cappella concerts on campus or have lectures in Memorial Hall or Sanders Theatre. And so poetry felt like part of the continuum. There was a room for it. And it felt like there was this connectivity.

Of course, within that, folks founded the Dark Room Collective— which I joined shortly after it began—to change that conversation about some of the things I think people in Boston took for granted about race or the centrality of X or Y voice. Some of those same conversations about inclusion and denial were at work then. Pushing the envelope was really important too, so I don't want it to seem like it was all roses or that the Woodberry Poetry Room changed poetry. But it did change my poetry. Like the Dark Room did for me, it provided a room of one's own that was outside of my personal room.

EH

The renovation of the poetry room drew criticism for its lack of fidelity to the original design, but more broadly, I'm curious about things inevitably getting lost in translation over time. Whether it's keeping up with technology or poetry through various archival methods or physical space through renovation or main-tenance or just age. I'm also thinking of the *New Yorker* piece you wrote about Ralph Ellison and the work he lost to fire. Drawing on your experiences working in archives and now a museum, I'm wondering about your thoughts on the preservation of a thing, a space, a feeling.

29

KY

The best archives are alive. The documents, the material, what have you. But there's also the physical archive. Many buildings have this symbolic importance, such as the Beinecke Library or the Schomburg Center, which was named a National Historic Monument when I joined as director. I remember walking down 135th Street, where the Schomburg Center is, to get some lunch one day, and there was an image of the building itself in the ground, like a plaque. That physical structure is so important in the imagination.

I don't know what the renovation of the Woodberry Poetry Room looks like, but I know there's always this balancing act. The National Museum of African American History and Culture building, which is five years old, in many ways feels like an entire piece of art. I would be horrified to know if someone adjusted the things that I think are its essence, but there are still parts we have to think about and add to and adjust. And with regards to the Woodberry Poetry Room, I can see how tricky it would be if you think of the room as an ensemble, which it certainly felt like, to move just one piece.

EH

I'm curious what you think is the essence of the museum.

KY

I honestly think it's the people and the collections together. The collections are central, but they don't matter if no one sees them. The essence is in the fact that we're able to bring people in to view themselves and each other and that the building is alive in that way. We just installed these important sculptures by Elizabeth Catlett, the African American artist who is so terrific and, fortunately for all of us, is all the more respected every day. They're these larger-than-life sculptures, and they change our first floor's Heritage Hall just by being there.

I'm on the side of the object and keeping the object as safe and original as possible. But I'm not on the side of never experiencing it, or never living in it, or keeping it in a drawer. Artifacts are meant to be shared. So, to me, that's the heart of the building. The building is a place where things happen. The building is so beautiful and majestic, I also think about the things and people that are in it and also the material those people collected and kept safe for so long.

The Woodberry Poetry Room was the same. It was about the poetry as much as the room as much as the feeling of the space and the people in it. And so I hope some of that at least is preserved.

EH

After some of the reflections you've shared today, would you want to go back and see it?

KY

I don't know. Now you got me curious.

Frankly, I hadn't thought much about the room recently until we started talking about it. And thinking about it again, I realized how central it was and how often I was there. I think a lot about how we make room for poetry in general and that other meaning of room, as in "accepted space." And I think that's really important. It's room for the humanizing moments you're talking about. I wouldn't say that it's just architecture or Aalto's design that does that in the poetry room. I think it's also poetry that seeks to think about the extraordinary and make the extraordinary an everyday experience. The Woodberry Poetry Room wasn't a grand room, but it had a grandeur to it. It wasn't a huge room, but it had a vastness to it. It contained a lot of poetry in the largest sense, and it turned out poetry as well. And there was something about that that let you know that you weren't alone and that other people had done this wild thing called writing poetry.

I just wanted to be part of poetry. Coming from Kansas and from my family in Louisiana, where I didn't know poets, I didn't totally know how to write poetry, but I knew that it was possible. I think those kinds of possibilities can't be taken for granted. Everything else you had to join or apply to. At Harvard there was always one more competition. And I purposely wouldn't join those things you had to "comp." I just wanted to write, you know? So, the poetry room was a place that provided access and, looking back, was one of many things that made the principle of access so important to me. You could just walk in. And I think there should be more of that quality in the world. Beauty shouldn't be so hard to come by.

31

Mindy Seu ⌐————————→ **Metahaven, "Inhabitant"** ⌐—
is a New York-based designer whose was a lecture given online at the
work reimagines the history of the GSD about notions of sensing and
internet and public engagement with inhabiting in filmmaking, art, and
digital archives. Seu is a graduate of design. It was delivered by Daniel
the MDes program at the GSD, where van der Velden of the Dutch design
she received the Design Studies Thesis practice Metahaven in October
Prize for her *Cyberfeminism Catalog*. 2020.
An updated manuscript is set to be
published by Inventory Press in 2022.

y Seu aven. itant"

33

———————————————————————————————————→ Andrea Sandell

ANDREA SANDELL

I want to start off by talking a bit about spreadsheets. I looked up your CV to prepare for this conversation, and I thought it was great how you present your own interests and research through this tool. I also thought of introducing something that isn't necessarily part of Metahaven's "Inhabitant" lecture but a bit closer to home for me. There is a series of drawings by Jan de Vylder and Inge Vinck that challenges the predominant understanding of spreadsheets as a tool made up of numbered frameworks. Within these frameworks we find a certain precarity: the anthropomorphized language of Excel, the infinite unraveling of the sheet, and the instruments of the medium that together open a space for fantasy. Is this tension between the coded and the Other something that resonates with your own understanding of graphics and design?

MINDY SEU

I love these examples because they document how we might subvert the intended use of the tool.

When digital spreadsheets first came out, they were considered functional programming for the masses. They were a liberatory technology with which anyone with a personal computer could undertake complex computation. The earliest digital spreadsheets appeared on Apple II on software called VisiCalc in the 1970s and on IBM's PC in the 1980s. They became even more popular when transformed into graphical user interface-based programs because people who did not know Terminal or Linux could understand what the spreadsheet functions meant. Things looked like buttons, cells and rows were denoted, and skeuomorphism① overtook the interface. This changed in part because spreadsheets have very two-dimensional x- and y-axes of rows and columns: they are confined structures that produce certain limits.

Rather than using the spreadsheet for something quantitative, the examples you shared take it as a drawing mechanism. They also remind me of some others who have been doing similar things with sheets. Danielle Aubert used spreadsheets as a canvas to draw something every day for a year, and Ramon Tejada used them to create an alternative history of graphic design because it was so easy for multiple users to add things at the same time.

But I do think part of the decoding you're talking about is figuring out how a tool is intended to be used and transgressing that use to a potentially greater end.

① Skeuomorphism refers to digital or interface design that mimics the qualities of real-world objects.

AS

Perhaps this is a transition into critically understanding the history of how these kinds of tools are created. Aesthetics opens an avenue through which to confront the design of information systems, whether these are spreadsheets, citations, or hyperlinks. Ted Nelson, whom you often cite, pioneered ways of understanding the limitations in how data structures index information.[2] How do you understand this history, and how do you position yourself within it, especially in your own work?

MS

Ted Nelson is considered the father of hyperlinks, hypertext, and a lot of other early digital technologies. Interestingly, his prototype ZigZag incorporated a z-axis into spreadsheets. Today we're accustomed to flatness in our conventional data structures, but by incorporating a z-axis, Nelson built multidimensionality into the page. Various connections can be made to the same cell rather than having to duplicate information. It was a kind of two-way link that allowed the user to access different data structures in a circular way.

Like many of his proposed tools, ZigZag didn't take off. But what I love about Nelson's thinking, and ZigZag especially, is its frustration with the limitations of what he calls "rectangularity and regularity." Such conventional data structures, especially tables and arrays, are confined structures created from a rigid, top-down specification that enforces regularity and rectangularity. By forcing people to systematize their content based on preexisting rows, columns, and taxonomies, there is no space for blurriness between those categories. Rather, his work encourages a multiplicity of voices and nonlinear readings. By building into our structures a dialectic of different opinions that bridge similarities and differences, we are allowed to build certain connections on our own.

As an influence on some of the things I'm thinking about, Nelson's work asks, "Okay, how do you actually let people develop their own taxonomies and ontologies? How do you allow people to embrace the blurriness between these categories?" And I feel like this also connects to Metahaven's reference to Anna Tsing's *The Mushroom at the End of the World* and concepts about interstitial spaces.

AS

How we might create in-betweenness is an extremely rich question, one that seems to develop two parallel yet interrelated dimensions: the network

35

[2] See Ted Nelson, *Computer Lib/ Dream Machines* (self-pub., 1974).

and the carrier bag. We can here cite Bruno Latour as a proponent of an ever-expanding notion of the social and adrienne maree brown as a proponent of inquiry through gathering.[9]

To bridge these two, Metahaven proposes the sponge as a deployable design object, one that functions as a vessel that contains its opposites, others, and fictions. I couldn't help but recall Ursula K. Le Guin's *Carrier Bag Theory of Fiction* and its reevaluation of the vessel as the first tool, a thesis that subverts the predominance of origin stories and the emboldening of individuals. Is the carrier bag your answer to Metahaven's question about what ways of sensing can we explore as inhabiting the present?

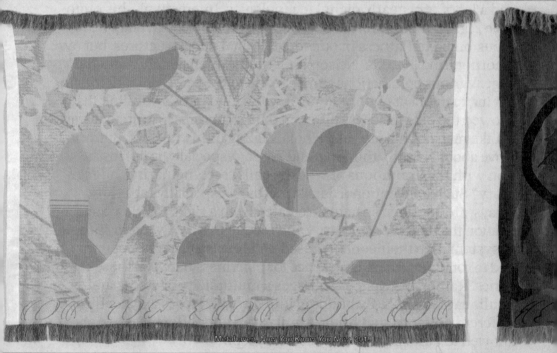

Metahaven, *Now You Know You Now*, 2019

Metahaven, "Inhabitant," October 5, 2020, Gund Hall Virtual Event Space, Harvard Graduate School of Design. Video still, 11:54.

MS

The two key ideas in that question are of senses and inhabitation: How can we situate ourselves in a space with our limited senses? I think Metahaven touched on a lot of the things that we lost and adapted to during the pandemic and how we're now trying to return to multisensorial space.

It is an interesting connection to the carrier bag, insofar as the carrier bag is really about inhabitants but perhaps less about sensing. In her short essay, Le Guin

[9] See Bruno Latour, *Reassembling the Social: An Introduction to Actor-Network-Theory* (Oxford: Oxford University Press, 2005), and adrienne maree brown, "Conversation Is Not a Master's Tool," The Scalability Project

creates an alternative history of technology in which the first tool is not the tool of dominance, the spear, but the tool of sharing, the basket. While both are useful for gathering food, the latter is intentionally meant as a form of harvesting and sharing among the community, while the former is rooted in violence and heroic linearity.

Le Guin's terms ask us to confront the ways we think about inhabiting space with technology today. By rethinking our first tool as one of sharing rather than dominance, how can we completely reframe what kind of tools we should be making and for what reasons? Communion supersedes individualism.

Sensing therefore becomes a multibodied process. It is not about one person inhabiting a space but rather about multiple people with multiple and varying senses gathering together as a commune. Inhabiting here signals being present and communing with each other, a process that adrienne maree brown articulates through the metaphor of the spider web: relationships can look diaphanous and tender while being extremely strong.

AS

It is. In the lecture, Daniel van der Velden presented Metahaven's design objects as things that lack singular definitions or overarching intentions. I like to think of their explorations as being ephemeral, and in this sense they behave like sponges: they don't have clear parameters or clear limitations embedded in the intention of their creation.

For them, sensing is the natural term or sensibility to refer to when developing these kinds of objects, a way of thinking that opens the surface of design to speculative potentials and veers away from the tendency to address preformulated problems.

MS

If you were to put a basket into a river, you wouldn't quite know what you'd get, but you might have an idea. This, I thought, was how Daniel talked about the way Metahaven think about videomaking. There's an interplay between control and letting go, being open to happenstance. And this is very different from a spear, where you have one thing in mind and you're targeting it. One is about a certain sort of waiting and wondering, and the other feels more deterministic.

AS

Can we then entertain a notion of gathering that works on a more critical level, in the sense of gathering not only images but also stories and representations?

MS

Yeah, absolutely! I do think gathering takes on two forms. The first is a material gathering, whether that's data or seashells or whatever you're collecting. The other is a social gathering, that is, the community that activates the collection or whatever has been aggregated.

AS

Does this resonate with your own approach to the Cyberfeminism Index, where in gathering content you find a sort of precarity engendered by the social?

MS

The precarity of the Cyberfem Index is apparent in its name: it is an open-ended term primarily constructed as an anti-definition. The prefix "cyber" first emerged with cybernetics, Norbert Wiener's concept of self-regulating mechanisms from the 1940s, and William Gibson attached "cyber" to "space" in his novel *Neuromancer*. This work was very much characterized by the male gaze and included things like fembots, cyberbabes, and Asiatic cyborgs that really perpetuated these racist and sexist stereotypes.

When I turned to feminism in '91, the field was questioning how marginalized communities might think of what cyberspace could be. Within this feedback loop, the question that emerged was about how we could be critical of the tool by using the tool itself. Many of these people were building online networks and building online tools and teaching hardware and software, all the while critiquing how cyberspace was used through its affordances or lack thereof.

This became more and more clear to me as I thought about the different physical manifestations of the Index. First, it was the spreadsheet, then it was my limited thesis publication at the GSD, and then the online site with Rhizome, and now the book being published this fall, which feels more official.[④] Through each iteration, different media revealed different holes in the Index.

The spreadsheet showed limitations in taxonomy, the online database in archiving, and the printed book in capturing movements and paths. These all build on top of each other, and it hopefully becomes clearer as each iteration evolves.

We can also connect ephemerality to archival spaces more broadly. Archives are like a clear slice of a history, with a clear agenda shaped by the curator or the gatherer. They are not meant to be representative of an entire historical moment, though they're often framed that way.

④ The printed publication *Cyberfeminism Catalog* will be published by Inventory Press in 2022.

Metahaven, *Elektra*, 2019

Metahaven, "Inhabitant," October 5, 2020, Gund Hall Virtual Event Space, Harvard Graduate School of Design, video still, 06:15.

Within the context of the Cyberfem Index, it feels quite precarious how many of the people included only partially exemplify or fit within this anti-definition.

39

Design like a Sponge

Metahaven, "Inhabitant," October 5, 2020, Gund Hall Virtual Event Space, Harvard Graduate School of Design, video still, 20:05.

Further, because it spans several decades, omissions, mistakes, and name changes make it ripe for human error. We embrace this; I don't think such an index will ever be complete. There will always be people who want to be excluded or included. There is a constant productive tension, which is compounded by the ephemerality of the indexed items themselves—digital artifacts, old images, old websites, untraceable quotes.

This leads to speculation: we're trying to frame how cyberspace might have been, which is a process of constant restructuring. What is in the archive now might degrade in a certain timeframe. This is also the charm of this type of archive, in that it encom-

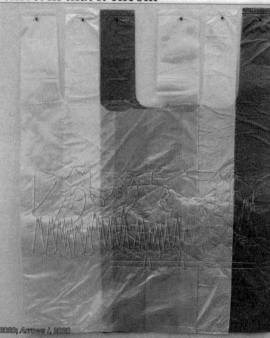

Metahaven, *Arrows II, 2020; Arrows I, 2020*

Metahaven, "Inhabitant," October 5, 2020, Gund Hall Virtual Event Space, Harvard Graduate School of Design, video still, 10:40.

passes both memory work and future-proofing. Who are we to say we can future-proof anything? I think we're just doing the best we can given the information we have now.

AS

On the one hand, precarity limits something's potential strength or decisiveness, but, on the other, it is the product of a desire to work against an inherited systematicity that might be limited or lacking. Can precarity therefore also be a tool for subversion, a tool to expand or work outside the limits of a given system or network, to escape institutional limitations?

MS

We can think of this evolutionarily: change or growth are caused by difference and variance. Difference and variance are vital. Even where there are many similarities, difference and variance actually allow for new modes of species- or relationship-building. In pointing us to Anna Tsing's work, Daniel was calling attention to the significance of embracing variance in what our processes collect.

Quoting Tsing, Daniel asked, "What if our time is ripe for sensing precarity? What if precarity, indeterminacy, and what we imagine as trivial are the center of the systematicity we seek? ... Stories built through layered and disparate pieces of knowing and being.

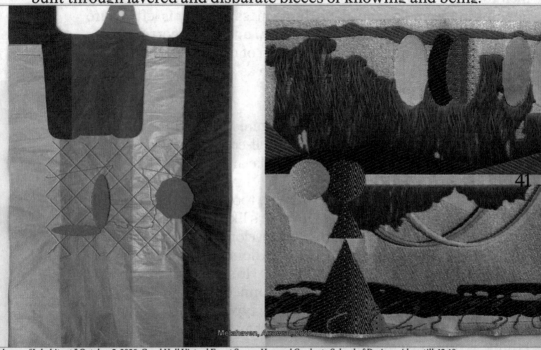

Metahaven, *Arrows I*, 2020.

Metahaven, "Inhabitant," October 5, 2020, Gund Hall Virtual Event Space, Harvard Graduate School of Design, video still, 12:40.

If the components clash with each other, this only enlarges what such stories can do."[5] In this mode, we direct our attention not to the big infrastructural moment but to the unsuspected. We allow the unsuspected and unplanned to prescribe what the intended use could be. Or rather, we try not to impose a single intended use but accept a multiplicity of what might emerge from these things.

I really like this idea of precarity in growth. How do we encourage spaces for variance and difference as we consider how this mode can be applied to larger groups of people?

[5] Anna Tsing, *The Mushroom at the End of the World: On the Possibility of Life in Capitalist Ruins* (Princeton, NJ: Princeton University Press, 2015), 20, 159.

AS

In a way, you're asking where the emancipatory potential might lie, right? I bring this up because it seems to point to a close interrelation between discursive objects' forms and content. The precarity of vessels or sponges lies in the thinning out of content.

In many aspects, Daniel's presentation was quite dense, and I appreciate your effort in working through this with me. Metahaven's work calls forth a series of appearances—cinematic, commercial, political, textual—across which they trace a network of interrelations. Nothing behind these appearances is set in stone, and therefore, their interrelations can be subverted. For Metahaven, at least, nothing remains in the end but an algorithmic mess. All that is left is pure substrate, something that is both critical and easily corruptible.

Have you ever entertained this notion of design research as a self-conscious art genre? Or of research as a type of criticism that subverts its own tools?

MS

I try to make tools in my practice. It's interesting to think about it as a self-conscious art genre. Part of that self-consciousness, I think, comes from questioning whether it is like art at all—perhaps that is not an interesting segue.

But I do think it's interesting to create tools and to be critical of the technology through the tool itself. It's like the cybernetic approach that I was so drawn to when developing the Cyberfeminism Index. And it's similar to what Daniel is doing too, specifying the differences between video and cinema. He's not claiming to abide by all the rules of cinema but instead connects it more to writing. He is basically trying to carve out a new type of genre: a proper research paper that happens to manifest as a moving image. This, I think, is quite fascinating.

Other artists, like Hito Steyerl, do this too, but Daniel sometimes gives us specific hints about what's going on. In one of the first images he shared—of makeshift hazmat suits—he made explicit his interest in the everyday incongruences between form and content. When people make hazmat suits out of recycled plastic bags and duct tape, there's no intention for them to be an artwork or a piece of fashion. The suits become art or fashion only when gathered, reclaimed, and inserted into a critical space. We may then begin to notice or question the actual incongruity or impromptuness.

This process creates a great distance between the gathered object and the original source. An impromptu act becomes a self-aware recreation in the attempt at criticality. I like this lens that Metahaven adopts: everything is driven and sustained by contradiction. It recalls our previous discussion on precarity. And, at the same time, Metahaven is willing to let their own presentation fall trap to this precarity: the argument unfolds in circles, through different examples.

As a corollary to this, we might look to ecological networks and other physical repercussions of what we consider to be quite ephemeral processes. In quoting Jennifer Gabrys, Daniel offered the camera sensor as a substitute for the camera lens: it works as a tool capable of sensing and gathering in Metahaven's cinematic approach. At the same time, he accepted the camera sensor's effect on how the nature scene unravels or unfolds in front of it. When inserted into nature, technology will naturally affect the actual natural context, not necessarily as a disruption but rather as an interjection. Even as we intend not to disturb an environment, the inclusion of a tool within it cannot avoid forming a new set of relations.

Thus, on the one hand, we might imagine a specific type of subversion: a broom can be used to sweep or, if you turn it upside down, to break a car window. On the other hand, we forget how the shape of the broom itself changes the shape of your hand. We always think that we are changing this environment without realizing that the environment is also changing our embodied experience. Within this latter sense, the subversion of tools within a practice can both reflect on the intended use of things and also encourage us to move away from such teleological frameworks. How can we uncover the precarity or breaking points of networks?

43

AS

Did you find that Daniel's lecture offered a position on these issues we've discussed?

MS

That is actually quite interesting—perhaps it did not. Daniel asked, "What ways of sensing can we explore as other ways of inhabiting the present?" And he presented various anecdotes as possible answers. Some of them were his own, but others were just his research. This created an associative reference base, which did not actually have a conclusion. There was no definitive outcome from this conjecture, and all we were left with were subverted interrelations.

Perhaps this is the proof of concept unto itself. Metahaven's work is asking what's possible, not offering the solution. Daniel did not seem to be solution-oriented, and even the people he mentioned, like Anna Tsing, are not solution-oriented thinkers.

AS

I completely agree. And yet I found myself reflecting on how we might make sense of a design project that embraces inconclusiveness as a way to open up a new, unregulated space.

Rather than being visual journalism with an emancipatory agenda, Metahaven's design project is a critical engagement with forms of state and social power. Over time, their agenda has lost an activist sense of determination and become markedly more ambivalent and harder to pin down as a political program.

Perhaps Metahaven sees design as now being too involved; all forms of power have become matters of design, an idea that finds its essential reference in the idea of network power. In this view, design has expanded its jurisdiction into geopolitical and economic networks. Not offering a conclusion to the lecture was a way to pull back from this tendency, to make us question whether design has radically expanded its jurisdiction.

MS

At the same time, the lecture employed a set of aesthetic and discursive strategies. These were somewhat speculative, insofar as they worked both as analysis and fiction. For example, Daniel began by talking about how video is more rooted in writing than in cinema. At the same time, he mentioned how he was likely not going to show many video clips because Zoom cannot handle that bandwidth.

The whole ensemble of case studies and self-references gave the lecture the feel of a piece of writing in progress or the unresolved research for some future manifestation. I wonder how he is planning on having this speculation manifest post-lecture because a lot of Metahaven's work is so cyclical and evolves from one form into another. And within the lecture itself, he talked about Zoom, compression algorithms, transmittance, and dissemination—all things Metahaven works with in practice.

Yeah, not to say that any of this will end necessarily, like it needs to have a thesis to be over, but I do think this work perhaps is not in its final form.

AS

I'm glad you returned to the beginning of the lecture. Daniel brought up how these projects are meant to be viewed, or at least how the public for these projects is formed. I think here of "public" in the sense critical theorist Nancy Fraser often employs, that is, of a space organized around a circulation of discourse rather than by a place or institution. Yet, for Metahaven, the site-specificity of the installation and the creation of a physical place of viewership are crucial. It affords them distance from the subject of their investigation. In the physical space, viewership is not a scroll, it is specific, undivided, and communal.

MS
It's a sort of worlding, right?

AS
Yes.

MS
Their work addresses a completely different environment, a completely novel context that we have not experienced, which is why it is ill-equipped for presentation in a movie theater or laptop screen. It has to be situated or immersed inside a world that they have created.

I was also struck by how in choosing for it to exist only in art spaces, Metahaven asks that the work be experienced almost nonlinearly or cyclically, because the viewer will very rarely go into a gallery and watch a video from the very start until the very end. So, what does it mean if you're entering at the middle and watching two minutes versus going up at the very end and looping back to the beginning? It really changes your understanding of the piece.

45

I like this approach because it reflects how we tend to consume information now. It is situated in a very specific context, and you

증거는 없고 오직 소문만 떠돈다.
No proof, only rumors.

우리는 반향이다.
We are reflections.

Metahaven, *Information Skies*, 2016

etahaven, "Inhabitant," October 5, 2020, Gund Hall Virtual Event Space, Harvard Graduate School of Design. Design, video still, 13:03.

Metahaven, *Eurasia (C*

Metahaven, "Inhabitant," October 5, 2020, Gund Hall Virtual Event Space, Harvard Graduate School of Design, video still, 06:38.

can either choose to delve in deeper or just skim the headline. I think those were two of the primary reasons why they choose to make the work site-specific.

s on Happiness), 2018

AS
I liked your term worlding. It makes me think that their work has
two different kinds of existence. One is in texts, and everything
else, anything that is image-based, can only exist in another world.

MS

I wonder if they're using the wrong language. Rather than focusing on video, they should, I think, describe the work as installation because the video was only one component of this larger set. And that isn't the case for a film in a theater. It's interesting that they focus so much on the content of the video and just glossed over the actual environment, which is a huge part of what they're doing.

AS

I like that we've ended on the specificity in which they present their work, the specificity of space. I'm curious how you envision equivalent or complementary spaces that exist digitally.

MS

This is why I think their work is the installation and not just the video. Together, those things create that world. I do think a website URL is also a world. Sometimes there is an interference—you might have multiple tabs open or something—but ultimately when you're going to a website, the expectation is that you're looking at the website. It's a contained experience. Same with a book: the book is a fixed, contained world that you enter.

I do wonder how this can be more malleable, if that's the intention. Do the other artworks in the gallery affect the way we perceive Metahaven's installation? Or, if we're annotating or inserting our own ideas into this fixed publication, do we not change that form? These questions of interactivity change the intended worlds that we enter into.

AS

I'm curious, have you seen or been near Metahaven's work before?

MS

Yeah. Because I was trained as a graphic designer, Metahaven was always this huge symbol. It was nice seeing this lecture though because it showed a lot of their newer works. Metahaven has shaped quite an important practice. There's always this question of the designer as X, but I feel like their practice is a very unique representation of the designer as researcher, artist, writer, etc.

It feels very multidisciplinary and strong.

Christopher C.M. Lee ⊂————→ **Smithsons' Golden Lane** ⊂————
is the Arthur Rotch Design Critic in was a 1953 urban housing competi-
the Department of Architecture at tion proposal for the City of London.
the GSD. He is the cofounder and Featuring a series of 16-story-tall
principal of Serie Architects in London, slab buildings linked by a network
Mumbai, and Beijing and has served of "streets in the sky," the proposal
as the Design Advocate for the Mayor focused on four distinct scales:
of London since 2017. His work is the house, the street, the district,
underpinned by the renewed relevance and the city. Although never built,
of typological reasoning and experi- the Golden Lane anticipated the
mentation to describe, conceptualize, Smithsons' Robin Hood Gardens
and project an idea of the city. and challenged post-war housing
typologies in England.

opher Lee

sons'

den
ne

→ Stephanie Rae Lloyd

STEPHANIE RAE LLOYD

Are you familiar with Alison and Peter Smithson's unbuilt 1952 proposal for the Golden Lane Estate? It was the ideological predecessor to Robin Hood Gardens, the housing project they designed in 1972, which marked the emergence of their idea for "the street in the sky." Both projects were located in London's East End neighborhood, a part of the city that was practically unrecognizable following the Second World War.①

CHRISTOPHER C.M. LEE

Yes, as familiar as one could imagine. You are absolutely right, it is difficult to look at Golden Lane and not discuss Robin Hood Gardens.

SRL

Did you ever have a chance to visit Robin Hood Gardens before it was partially demolished in 2017?

CL

Yes, I did. It was notorious.

SRL

What was your impression? Considering its reputation among the public as a failure, what did you think of it as an architect?②

CL

Robin Hood Gardens was notorious for many reasons. A lot of things failed. First, the buildings flanked the street with two concrete walls, each one-story high, that separated the street from the site, producing almost bunker-like conditions. Second, rather than activating the street edge, the Smithsons erected, as you mentioned, streets in the sky. These streets were quite deep in the section, so they didn't get much sunlight, and many of them terminated in dead ends. Third, the design was intended to foster Jane Jacobs's edict, "eyes on the street." However, the streets in the sky at Robin Hood Gardens operated quite differently from, let's say, a street on the ground, which carries a lot of other pedestrians that are not only from the housing estate but from the wider city.

There was a certain distance traveled between the designs of the Golden Lane Estate and Robin Hood Gardens. Although

① During the 20th century, English society viewed the East End with suspicion and fascination. The term "the East End" was used pejoratively, beginning in the late 19th century, as the expansion of London's population led to a high concentration of poor people and immigrants in this part of the city, who faced extreme overcrowding and generally unhealthy living conditions.

② "The access to the building is, to our mind, ill-conceived: the 'stress-free' zone is abused: the lack of common privacy is a constant worry: the vicious writing-on-the-wall is hard to ignore, and is undeniably related to much of the mindless vandalism that has broken down the communal facilities. The tenants do not make use of the decks and, consequently, the idea of 'street' does not have any factual validity. . . [Our] final assessment must be that, socially, the building does not work. The lucidly argued Smithson aesthetic fails at Robin Hood." John Furse, "The Smithsons at Robin Hood" (PhD diss., University of Sussex, 1982).

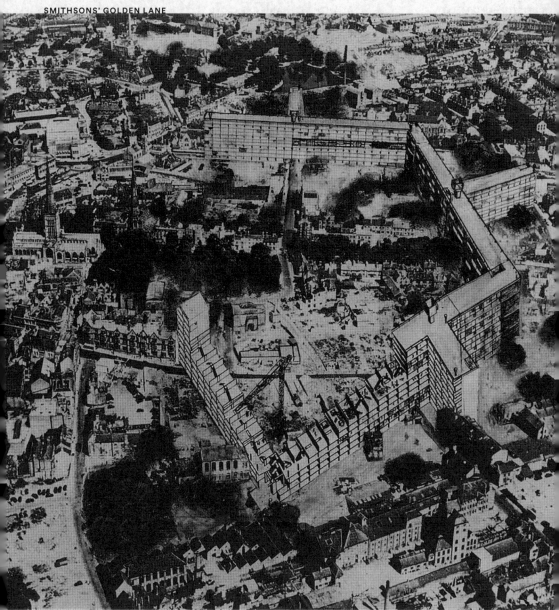

otomontage showing the planned construction process for the Golden Lane Estate. The housing complex was designed to be erected using a tower ne, which was not then used in the United Kingdom. Alison and Peter Smithson, Golden Lane Estate, London, 1952.

the idea of the building as a street in the sky is very much present in both, the placement of the street was critically different. In Golden Lane, the circulation "twigs" essentially cut the site diagonally. The building did not define the edge of the site, which is a standard in housing today.

SRL

I want to quickly jump into a discussion of "type" as a way to set up this conversation about Golden Lane as it relates to standards in contemporary housing projects. "Type" in architectural discourse is commonly considered a formal or programmatic classification of the built environment. As I learned in your Spring 2021 option studio and as you discuss in your writing, understanding type through use tells us little about the shared characteristics of the artifacts that belong to the group in question, impeding the knowledge that you could have acquired otherwise. Can you speak to how type can be understood as an idea rather than a model?

CL

I think type as an idea rather than a model comes from the 18th-century French archaeologist and architectural theorist Antoine-Chrysostome Quatremère de Quincy, who was the first to introduce the word into architectural discourse. Quatremère de Quincy

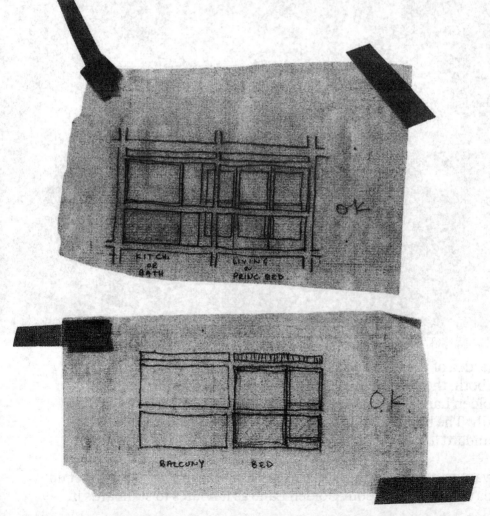

Initial sketches of facade designs according to interior rooms. Alison and Peter Smithson, Golden Lane Estate, London, 1952.

defined "type" as an idea that should rule over the model, which is to say that we have an idea that we all hold in common, and that idea guides us to create further iterations of that very idea.

A good way to explain it is with Plato's idea of "bed."[9] For Plato, while there is a commonly held idea of what constitutes the ideal bed, it is impossible to produce a perfect model of bed, which is why endless variations of bed exist. The idea is something that rests in our minds. Quatremère de Quincy placed less importance on the physical characteristics of bed and more importance on the agreed upon understanding of the idea of what constitutes bed.

SRL

So these typological ideas that we hold in common can never fully materialize?

[9] In Book X of *The Republic*, Plato tells of Socrates's metaphor of the three beds: one bed exists as an idea made by God (the Platonic ideal); one is made by the carpenter, in imitation of God's idea; and one is made by the artist in imitation of the carpenter's idea.

[10] "This search for what is common in the city—through architecture— has been underpinned by the discursive definition of the typical. This search arose in critical moments of architectural history, at points where architecture was forced to redefine its role and relevance in a context affected by societal, economic, and political changes and demands . . . . In the conception of the modernist city, the notion of the typical came to be identified with the standard. The typical or standard object came to provide a framework for a social and ideological agenda that informed the design and production of all artefacts to encompass life . . . . The city was read as something that constantly evolved and changed, and thus what was crucially permanent was ultimately typical. . . . Through this search and redefinition of the typical, I would argue that the recourse to the city as a project to revalidate the works of architecture is underpinned by the redefinition of what constitutes the common. In other words, what will be the idea of the city that architecture must again respond to?" Christopher C.M. Lee, "The Idea of the City," *Midtown, Midrise, Mid-door*, Spring 2021.

CL

Exactly. If we think of type as an idea that produces further variation, it opens up to interpretation. It also allows those involved in the making and designing of a set of standards, paradigms, or bases to discuss, compare, and evaluate.

SRL

I'm thinking about the potential implications of this understanding of type in architectural discourse. If designers can never physically produce these ideals, why do we keep trying? Perhaps our role as architects lies precisely in the ability to identify what is common.

CL

It's less about whether the pursuit of producing the physical manifestation of the ideal is important. What is more important is that the heuristic value of type allows us to revalidate the cultural, social, and political dimensions of architecture.[10] Type here is used as a heuristic device rather than as a formal procedure to create further variations. Thinking in this manner allows us to question the ideas we collectively hold in common.

55

SRL

The Smithsons were directly responding to the work of Le Corbusier and Ludwig Mies van der Rohe; their work can be read as part of a collective questioning of mid-century cultural ideals. Where I believe the Smithsons departed from Le Corbusier and Mies, however, is in their specific attention to questioning what was contextually common, perhaps because they were working within the pressing postwar conditions in the UK. The way I read Golden Lane is as a great example of the Smithsons' attempt to revalidate the common. Despite the fact that the project was never built and never shaped the physical space of the city, the ideas of the project continue to endure in contemporary housing projects.

CL

You open up very interesting avenues for looking at the Smithsons' work.

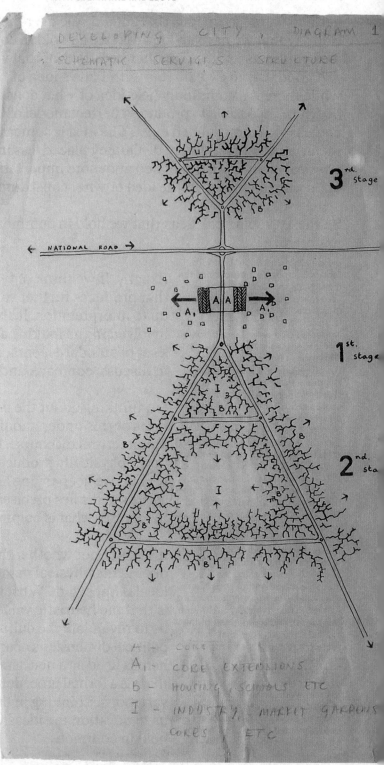

Competition drawings of distant views seen from Golden Lane. Alison and Peter Smithson, Golden Lane Estate, London, 1952.

As I understand it, their work has not been discussed in reference to notions of type. Discussing architecture through type means looking at the transformation of building types, as well as the architecture that has persisted, in order to embed new meaning or understanding in the architecture of today.

You're absolutely right to say that the Smithsons brought together ideas from architectural modernism to London's East End, which had one of the highest concentrations of council housing at the time.[5] Golden Lane borrows some of the lessons and inventions of architectural modernism, but it also deviates from them. For example, Golden Lane differs from the work of Le Corbusier because it recognizes that the city should be built incrementally. It produces a cluster city, which is essentially a network of buildings that produces a twig-like arrangement of housing blocks that grow organically over time. These twig-like arrangements loosely frame the open common spaces below and do not have an underlying grid to which it must adhere ad infinitum.

Where I think the Smithsons departed from the modernists was in consciously introducing the idea of the everyday, the ordinary, or the "as found." They imbued architectural modernism with the lived experience of everyday life. They tried to adapt architectural modernism to fit within the postwar 1950s context. In theorizing objects "as found," they allowed anything and everything to be raised in association with architectural ideas. They were also very influenced by the work of English photographer Nigel Henderson, who was well known for documenting ordinary conditions within London's East End. To be obsessed with the everyday life of the East End would have been alien to Le Corbusier.

The ideas we find in the early work of the Smithsons and their Golden Lane proposal, including this idea of "as found," permeate throughout their work and architectural discourse for at least two decades after the proposal was completed.

SRL

I'm personally interested in the Smithsons because I feel as though they represent a historical counternarrative to other canonical examples of architectural modernism, precisely because they were preoccupied with the common or the ordinary. It's always confusing to me why the academy holds onto Mies and Le Corbusier when there exist examples like the Smithsons. While I agree that it's important to understand these canonical theories and buildings in order to move

57

[5]"Council housing" refers to public housing in the United Kingdom or to housing owned by a local authority.

forward, I hope that we can expand the boundaries of architectural discourse in order to center figures like the Smithsons, especially because they were directly in dialogue with other canonical figures during this time.

CL

I think the way in which we are discussing the Smithsons is actually unusual. People don't usually make this connection between the heuristic value of type and the revalidation of architectural modernism through the Smithsons. If Rossi looked at Palazzo della Ragione, then the Smithsons looked at the East End.

SRL

The Smithsons were incredibly influential in England during this time.[6] Through both their written and built work they popularized what became known as New Brutalism. But this new aesthetic amassed loads of public criticism.[7] Why do architects love the Smithsons' work but the public does not?

[6] "Virtually the only British architects to have an international reputation and whose influence on architecture since the war has been out of all proportion to the relatively small amount of their work to be built." *The Smithsons on Housing*, produced by B.S. Johnson, BBC Two, July 10, 1970.

[7] Timothy Hyde, "Irritation," *Ugliness and Judgment: On Architecture in the Public Eye* (Princeton, NJ: Princeton University Press, 2019).

[8] "Midtown, Midrise, Mid-door" considered three recent and significant shifts in the design of collective housing in London: "Midtown" addressed the changing nature of workspace and their related amenities brought about by the pandemic; "Midrise" dealt with the potential for carbon neutral construction offered by cross laminated timber structures; and "Mid-door" challenged the "fabric-first approach" of Passivhaus in housing design. "Type and the Idea of the City: Architecture's Search for What is Common" considered the theoretical and historical understanding of type as a heuristic device in the discourse of the city as a project. Taking Anthony Vidler's "The Third Typology" as a starting point, the seminar proposed a fourth typology as a common framework for the production of an architecture of the city in today's globalized context.

CL

Just after the war, architecture in the UK was still seen as a very gentlemanly profession. The English being the English, there was a certain reasonableness that eschewed the avant-garde, manifestos, or big proclamations. What is unique about the English, maybe especially during that time, was precisely this lack of posture, and that agreeableness was still persistent. It's very English and hard to understand.

SRL

Perhaps it's an argument for a postureless position?

CL

The posture is the lack of posture. So given this context, the Smithsons were radical.

SRL

I'm thinking about your Spring 2021 option studio, "Midtown, Midrise, Mid-door," as well as your seminar course, "Type and the Idea of the City," both of which directly address this question of type.[8] You claim that these courses also work typologically and that historical precedent is a crucial

Photomontage with Gérard Philipe. Alison and Peter Smithson, Golden Lane Estate, London, 1952.

component of your teaching methodology. Can you elaborate on the benefits of working in that manner?

CL

These courses were based on Rossi's contribution to the way in which we draw on the persistent architecture of the city, which required a certain awareness of the ideas still held in common within the city or the site in order to design a proposal. Of course, this was complemented by the realization that architectural knowledge can also be drawn from itself. In these courses, we tried to make a case for not mapping arbitrary conditions but instead selecting architectures that we felt were relevant to the site and context in which we were working. By working this way, we were able to compare various examples of architecture or buildings that share similar characteristics, either physical or ideal. From there, it was a process of abstraction.

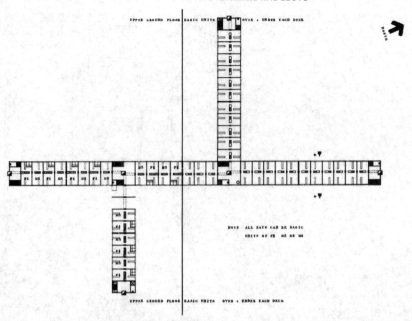

Upper ground floor plan. Alison and Peter Smithson, Golden Lane Estate, London, 1952.

Whereas Rossi simply looked at architecture of the historical European city, in these courses we sampled projects on a global scale in order to produce a comparative analysis of type.

Unlike Rossi, we belong to a generation that is global; our collective knowledge is not bound by one site, one continent, or one city. We come from different places and our makeup is the sum of our learning and experience within those different places. Working in a global city allows us to be absolutely contextual in order to see the persistent type in the city. But also, we are able to draw upon architectural examples that we feel share the same characteristics or ideas, though they perhaps have a different deep structure.[⊚] There are also examples that have the same deep structure but perhaps have a different idea altogether. I think it's this collision that we found most productive as a means to conduct the studio. It's also in a sense further from what Rossi has done. If Rossi was all about the historical city, we were more interested in the global city.

SRL

That's interesting because your own practice, Serie, is quite global. Do you implement this methodology of analyzing typology into your professional work?

CL

⊚ Deep structure is the common organizing principle of an architectural type.

Yes, absolutely. That's why I think, as best as possible, we teach what we practice, and we practice what we teach. Our generation is unlike the previous generation. Norman Foster is a good example of someone from the previous generation who worked his early days in England, amassed a very large portfolio, and then exported that style elsewhere through his work as Foster + Partners.

Whereas when we started our studio first in London and Mumbai, and then in Singapore and Beijing, we found ourselves working in disparate locations without a large portfolio. It was very liberating but also very daunting because we wanted to be sure that the work that we produced in each location had a deep understanding of or contextual relevance to the site.

We didn't want to exoticize that which is not Western by playing on the clichés of the vernacular. We really didn't want to exoticize the local context. Therefore, we thought that we must first assess the ideas that are held in common within our context and the context within which we were working.

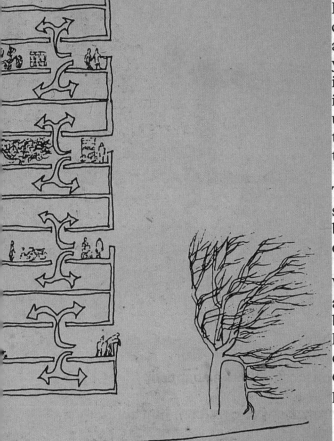

SRL

Does working typologically free you from appropriation? Because you're not simply stealing techniques, you are instead analyzing and understanding the cultural motivation behind the architecture?

CL

That's right. You're understanding the reasoning behind the persistence of architectural spaces.

SRL

We touched on type as a heuristic device a little bit earlier. To me, it seems like a tool for building cultural consensus. What does that look like in practice? How does—

61

tional diagram. Alison and Peter Smithson, Golden Lane Estate, London, 1952.

Photomontage of a deck or a street in the sky. Alison and Peter Smithson, Golden Lane Estate, London, 1952.

CL

Do we hold a vote or a referendum?

SRL

Yeah, exactly. How does this consensus building happen?

CL

The consensus happens not through a vote or referendum but is

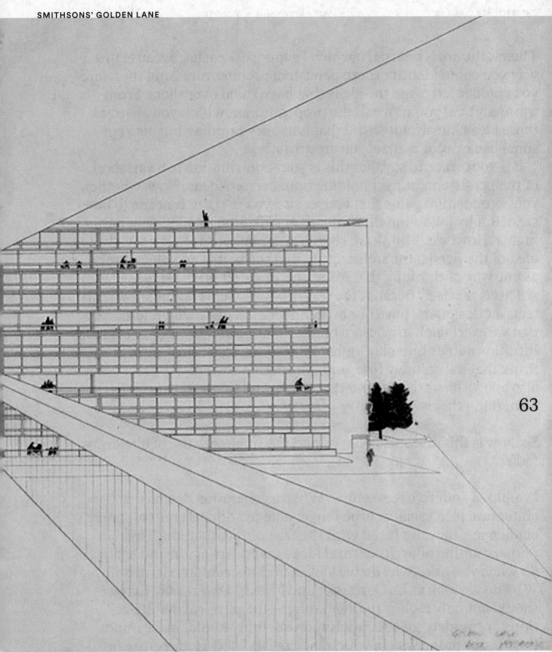

implied (and read) through persistent architecture. If an architecture persists, it means that its relevance is continued. That its relevance is still valid. Otherwise, that "type" of architecture will cease to be built.

SRL

But that implies quite a bit of time. Waiting to see if something persists is a very slow process.

CL

There's the analytical part, which I suppose is easier, because in a way you could identify these persistent architectures and therefore you could interrogate the ideas that have ruled over them. From the analytical you move to the proposition in which you abstract these ideas into architecture that is at once familiar, but also personal because, of course, you are an author.

It is your voice to say that this is your contribution to a variation of the persistent, but yet holding onto certain ideas. Now, whether your proposition gains that consensus, you're right, it needs to be seen. But by following this process, the likelihood of persistence is higher. However, I think we should also not confuse, let's say, the idea of the persistent architecture and the heuristic value of type as one way of thinking that insists upon a smooth continuity.

This is precisely because the way in which we, as authors, as architects, as designers, have our own tendencies, our own preferences that we exert upon in a design process that cannot be fully explained. Intuition comes into play, right? Preference comes into play. But I think that's absolutely fine, and I think that's wonderful because it also allows for variation, interpretation, and richness to arise from something that is common.

SRL

So, how is this discourse on type and the architect's use of it relevant today?

CL

I would say our role is essential. When a generation deems that architecture is in crisis or is no longer able to address contemporary challenges, they are faced with the task of revalidation. This re-questioning of architectural ideas reappears again and again. So when you ask, "why do we look at architectural modernism? Why do we look at Le Corbusier and Mies?," I would say that we should not only look at their buildings—the physical manifestations or "models" of their architecture—but should, more importantly, look at the way in which they revalidated architecture to make new claims. That's the critical leap we should aim to understand so that we can in turn make a similar leap. It's absolutely fundamental for each generation to understand so that they can make a claim for their own architecture.

Thomas Demand ⟵——————⟶ **Blaschka Glass Flowers** ⟵
is a German sculptor working between   is a collection of plant models crafted
Berlin and Los Angeles whose work   meticulously out of colored blown
is exhibited worldwide. His one-to-one   glass by the Bohemian glassworkers
scale paper models, which he photo-   Leopold and Rudolf Blaschka in Dresden,
graphs in his studio, often reference   Germany, between 1890 and 1936.
familiar images circulated through   Originally commissioned by the Harvard
mass media. He currently teaches at   Botanical Museum as a teaching
the Hochschule für bildende Künste   collection, today they are on public
Hamburg in Germany.   display at the Harvard Museum of
                                         Natural History.

mas and

and

ehka

ss

vers

————→ Olivia Howard

Black-and-white photograph of the Blaschka glass plant models.

OLIVIA HOWARD

The importance of looking closely is something you've mentioned regarding your own work, and the Blaschkas, too, observed plant specimens very carefully to create their glass models. They didn't work from an intermediate image, such as a photograph, for example.

THOMAS DEMAND

Right, the Blaschkas really wanted to represent three-dimensional objects as they saw them. Something I really appreciate about their work is that you think differently with your hands than you do with your eyes and brain. When you do something mechanically, you understand, you analyze, you have ideas, you have techniques, and you have to find solutions. Thinking with the hands was very important for the Blaschkas. Making an object, realizing how it actually works, and the ways in which all its different parts interact with each other is a way of analyzing the plant itself. The camera doesn't do that. I still think of photography as a very reliable tool for representing things, but science has known for a long time that it leaves out the most interesting parts of the research.

The Blaschkas came from a 19th-century scientific context, which was very different from our current cultural context. At the time of its invention, in the early to mid-1800s, photography was a purely mechanical and rather unreliable tool. The analytic potential of the eye was still far superior to that of a photographic lens, which flattened everything. That's why these glass models, as a teaching collection, have a real advantage over standard drawings, illustrations, or lithographs, which only show the plant from one side. A famous photographic reference from the period is Karl Blossfeldt's black-and-white photographs observing the life of plants, which were highly influential but also highly ornamental.[1] They concern the wonders that nature can bring to macrophotography and the tools of photography, such as the grayscale and the geometric value of a good, large lens. But regarding the plants themselves, they are mute. All of this gets in the way for the Blaschkas, I think.

OH

In what context did you first become familiar with the Blaschkas' work?

69

TD

Fifteen years ago, in Monaco, I was working on a show called *La Carte d'apres Nature* about our representation of nature.[2] Naively, I was hoping that I could get a few of the Blaschkas' glass sea creatures on loan from the Oceanographic Museum in Monaco City. The museum is a big and pompous educational building that drops from a cliff down into the sea. They had several Blaschka chandeliers and glass ornaments and some glass jellyfish on view in their exhibits as well. The jellyfish were quite interesting in that they resisted being decorative—and they were beautiful!

[1] Karl Blossfeldt, *Acanthus mollis (Soft Acanthus, Bear's Breeches. Bracteoles with the Flowers Removed, Enlarged 4 Times)*, 1898–1928, Thomas Walther Collection at the Museum of Modern Art, New York. See moma.org, digital image.

[2] *La Carte D'Après Nature*, curated by Thomas Demand, New National Museum of Monaco, Villa Paloma, Monaco, September 18, 2010– February 22, 2011.

OH

Actually, George Lincoln Goodale, the director of the Harvard Botanical Museum, first saw the Blaschkas' marine invertebrates in the Museum of Comparative Zoology, which is how he came to the idea to commission the glass flowers from them.[3]

TD

I mean, it's a genius idea because you can't really see jellyfish. Especially not in the 19th century. Today you can see them with ultraviolet light, but at the time, it was just the most brilliant idea to make them out of glass.

OH

Exactly. The Blaschkas rendered visible what was then unattainable. On the other hand, the species of flowers in our collection are rather commonplace in the Americas and Europe. Most of them are actually weeds. Isn't it then a curious practice to model them in such great detail, with such precision?

TD

The Blaschkas didn't have a photographic idea of the world. They were educated in the 19th century's Romantic sensibilities of painting, drawing, and visual arts. I think of the models as three-dimensional drawings rather than scientific, photographic, or mechanical reproductions. The Blaschkas were quite lyrical. If you look at the arc of a plant stem as it lays there, of course it looks natural. But they could have rendered it in a blunt way too, and it would be just as scientifically valid. Instead, they have this romantic little curve. This is important because, at the time, people used art to depict nature in an innocent way, without being representative of God or a feudal system. Suddenly, a Romantic painter would draw a tree with all the leaves, which would take ages, but would not show the shepherd underneath or Diana bathing. It was just a tree as a marvel in itself. I think the Blaschkas were coming from that seminatural sense of wonder.

③ From 1886 to 1936, Leonard and Rudolph Blaschka produced a series of colored glass models of plants and flowers. The glass models were commissioned as a teaching collection by George Lincoln Goodale, who was a botanist and founding director of the Harvard Botanical Museum. In his instruction of botany students, Goodale sought a way to preserve the color and form of flowers, which were lost when pressed in a herbarium or submerged in liquid. Having observed the Blaschkas glass models of marine invertebrates, on display in the university's Museum of Comparative Zoology, Goodale pursued the father-and-son glassworkers to apply their techniques to plant biology.

OH

This is a teaching collection, so the models have been photographed numerous times to make slides and transparencies that can communicate across the classroom. But in many cases, you look at these photos, and they might as well be photographs of the plant itself.

TD

Yes, photographs of the models still don't tell you much about the flowers, even whether or not the flowers are made of glass. The most important thing that I see in them is the notion of still-standing time. The still lives you know from Dutch art history, for example, are all about the Rococo or food that will be rotting soon, which is a fleeting luxury to have. Representations of fruit or flowers are always about the moment of perfection, right before they turn. To take them out of that cycle and create a fresh flower that lasts forever—a flower that is fairly close to the real sensation of the real flower—is unique and remark-

.ck-and-white photograph of a glass model by the Blaschkas and a real flower. On the left is the real flower, and on the right is its glass replica.

able, a fantastic object in the sense of phantasmagoria. At the same time, the object is super fragile and cannot be carried around. These two elements together are peculiar and philosophically very rich.

OH

Speaking of still lifes, I wonder if you noticed the Blaschka series *Fruits in Decay*, of rotting pears, strawberries, and apples. As you mentioned, the Blaschkas also modeled moldy fruits and studied very closely the ways in which they rot, complicating the concept that they are flowers that never fade.

TD

I consider decay, on the one hand, a type of Mannerism, and on the other, in more philosophical terms. The most beautiful stage of life suddenly depends on your concept of beauty. Is the most beautiful flower the one that's ripest and on the edge of decay, at its highest point, from which it will only go downhill? Is that the best moment? Or is it the flower that is just about to open? These questions represent different concepts of what beauty means in nature and serve to paraphrase life in general. So, I think that's a Mannerist quality that the Blaschkas can get away with, but at the same time, it's a central topic of art history. And they were very educated in that,

Lantern slide of a glass model of a great bougainvillea flower.

OH

Perhaps we could talk about models on their own? You often refer to the model as a cultural technique that describes its broader function. For example, some models are more abstract, such as those used in physics, or they can quite literally be miniatures, like dollhouses. Something that is particular about this collection of models is that the models are full-scale or even enlarged to show greater detail. What potential does one-to-one scale afford the model?

TD

The most convenient way for the Blaschkas to have made the instructional models was to make them bigger, so that students

Bidens laevis
LARGE BUR-MARIGOLD   58
BROOK SUN FLOWER

73

wouldn't need magnifying glasses. I can't see a simple reason why they would have made them smaller because that would diminish the educational effect and make things more difficult or ornamental. I think the enlargement is interesting. It's the same for me. I just don't know what a miniaturization of the world would mean, other than making things neater. In the broader cultural field, people are starting to understand that models are equally as interesting as icons and images. Models act as filters to a reality that is way too complex and that we can't understand all at once. And, in that sense, it's very familiar to look at a model because it leaves out things which are not important to its particular purpose and emphasizes other, more important things.

If you make a model smaller, it has a dollhouse aesthetic and can no longer be taken seriously. I want to avoid that by all means. Otherwise you would say "Oh! How cute!," and that would be about it. You stop thinking. The purpose of my work is obviously very different from the Blaschkas', but in that sense, we're very close. Also, the ways in which their models catch the light really brings them to life. A flower petal has translucency, and the lucidity of colored glass is so amazing. It should be fun to look at them. Look at all these details! Look at how complex a flower is! That makes them educational, too, because it should be fun to study rather than burdensome. And same with my models! They should be fun to look at.

OH

They're very fun to look at! As for your work, you only model at one-to-one scale.

TD

One-to-one scale is the only way to make a proper model that comes close to your own experience and can transmit that experience. When it comes to a city, it's different. It would be nonsense to build Rome in the year 100 BCE at a one-to-one scale. In general, anything smaller than one-to-one doesn't do anything for me. Part of modeling is getting into the detail, the atmosphere, the character, the biography—however you want to name it—of a space. I know that I need to have a certain specificity in my sculptures to propose to the viewer that someone has been there or to represent a situation where people have been working, sleeping, moving around, or where someone may have even been killed! I need to show that it's a place where something is happening.

OH

At the GSD, we're especially keen to know more about your interest
in architectural models in particular. Can you speak about your
relationship with the world of architecture?

TD

The architecture world took note of my work very early on. There
were studio courses where they would make models "in the manner
of Thomas Demand," an activity in which, by the way, I was never
involved. There have also been competitions by architecture firms
that would reference my work, such as Kersten Geers and David
Van Severen's Belgian Pavilion at the Venice Biennale.④ I could tell
that there was a certain interest in my way of understanding light,
atmosphere, and surface in interior spaces. I was happy to see that
because architeture is, as you know yourself, full of discourse,
which is often about what architecture should do. Take photography,
on the other hand. Susan Sontag, one of the canonical writers on
the medium, did not write about what photography is for. She wrote
about what photography means and about distinctions between
one type of photograph and another. She wrote about photography's
relationship to truth. I don't see those kinds of abstract issues in
architectural discourse. Maybe that's why I feel drawn to it as well.   75
There is nobody telling me, "What you're doing is nonsense!" [laughs].
And so far, my work in architecture has been enormously fun, and
I have been surrounded by enormously talented people. I think the
people I've had the pleasure to work with are some of the best.

OH

The very best, yes. As a student, your work was introduced to me
in the context of interior models, in their concern with representing
space, being able to see it, analyze it, and critique it. But what's
happening in your images is very different. I think that in architecture there is a strong desire to make powerful images, and at the
point where we are now technologically, we're a bit disillusioned
with this hyperrealistic, glossy, colorful, digital-rendering aesthetic.
I think that we're looking for a visual language that means something to us. Perhaps that's one aspect of your work that interests us.

TD

That's another parallel with photography. The ability to manipulate
a mediocre photograph into a stunning one is very easy with software. It's like plastic surgery. People don't find an end. They do too

④ *After the Party*, Belgian Pavilion,   much, and they keep doing it until the
11th Venice Architecture Biennale,   face looks like any other face and be–
September 14–November 23, 2008.

comes ugly. The extra detour I take by making a model of a space, which other architects very often do too, involves acknowledging the fact that software takes over too much. The process of designing is super easy, and technology is amazing, but it also creates a distance between you and the object you're designing. And as I said, thinking with your hands is very different from thinking with a screen.

OH

In your work, you deal with aspects of abstraction and simplification at the architectural scale. The space that you're modeling at full scale extends beyond the frame. Is there a difference in the way that you handle the specificity of objects as opposed to spatial volumes?

TD

No, I'm trying to boil down most of the different materials into one material, one surface. In that sense, I'm paraphrasing painting. If you do an oil painting, everything will be pictured in oil and made of oil paint. In photography, the lens loves to capture microstructures and different shades and nuances. However, I'm basically refusing many of the main features of photography as part of my work because I use the same flat surface for everything. And, to a certain degree, I want to prevent my images from becoming too illusionistic. There should always be this weird effect that you cannot unsee once you see that it's not real. I wouldn't use marbled paper to represent Carrara marble, for instance. That would be going too far, and that's not really what I'm after. I'm trying to make an idealized rendering of a very banal place, one that has a certain significance in a context which, simply put, I know that you know. Not a simple sentence, but it's a simple transaction, basically.

OH

Well put. It's not always your own sculptures that you photograph though, you also collaborate with architects.

TD

Yes, I photograph other people's models too. I photographed a series of models by SANAA for a show that just opened at the Garage Museum of Contemporary Art in Moscow.[9] I call them "model studies" because I literally look at them, photograph them, and frame them. SANAA does one-to-one scale tests of everything, of every cable channel on a steel facade, for instance, to show how they wrap around a steel pillar. Or, for the corrugated metal panels used for the roofing, they want to see the exact color.

[9] Thomas Demand, *Mirror Without Memory*, Garage Museum of Contemporary Art, Moscow, September 10, 2021–January 30, 2022.

L. & R. Blaschka, No. 99, 1889.

OPUNTIA CAMANCHICA, Engelm&Bigel.
Comanche Cactus.

Western Kansas, Colorado to Texas and Arizona.

...notype of a Comanche cactus glass model.

It's not about getting a sample from the manufacturer. They really want to design a structure in the best possible way, visualizing every detail that is significant for them in one-to-one. The models are mostly made in cardboard and paper because that's the easiest to get rid of afterwards, but they are a very touching and beautiful validation of my own practice.

OH

77

That's a rare meeting point between your practices. Not many offices work in this way.

TD

SANAA uses these models to communicate within the office, which is multilingual. Much of the conversations with American and German and Russian architects, etc., happen through the model, going through 50 different variations of the same idea, until they find the right shape. Especially if you look at the undulating shapes, which are very hard to create. I mean, anyone can make a curve, but it will be weak. You can see this in Zumthor's extension to the LACMA in Los Angeles.© The first shapes he made were not strong and they didn't represent the tension in the structure because he's not used to that kind of form. Now they look much more refined. Muscular, even. You can tell that SANAA are masters at finding a curve that is not coincidental or weak or soft. I think most of it comes through making models.

© Peter Zumthor, Resnick Pavilion at the Los Angeles County Museum of Art, Los Angeles, 2020–present.

You know how sometimes SANAA's thin steel roofs sag between the columns of their buildings? I thought this was because of an error in construction. That's why other people make really thick roofs, so that they don't sag. But no, they actually saw the same sag when looking at the model, and they said, "We want it sagging, too." They built the real thing to behave in the same way a piece of paper would behave. That is not only charming, it's also subversive, really, to the whole idea of stability in architecture. And those ideas again come through modeling. Having a sense, talking about it, seeing it, making it for yourself. As for me, I still make my models for myself. Then the photograph follows, acting as a window into the studio, so you can actually see what I'm doing. But for me the most important thing is the object I make in the context of other objects. When do they obtain narrative potential? When do they get specific enough?

OH

In reference to the SANAA roofs that sag between the columns, this seems to be a moment where the model and the "real" building become one. Do you think that your interest in architectural practice and discourse has brought you closer to this crossover? Is there a desire to design an architectural space yourself?

TD

I'm actually doing that at the moment. Caruso St John Architects and I are building a pavilion for the headquarters of Kvadrat in rural Denmark. It's located at the end of the world. If you want to go there and have a meeting with them about your product or negotiate a deal, you have to travel to Copenhagen, and from there to Aarhus, and then get in a car for an hour. You can't make it back to wherever you came from on the same day. They wanted it to be a destination as much as a business. If someone travels all that way, they should leave with a good memory. I think that's a fine purpose for a building, but it also means that not many people will see it in the flesh. So, in a weird sense, it will be very consistent with my other work, because it will mostly live through photographs. However, in this project, the role between me and the architects is reversed. I design the entire thing, and they communicate the necessities, make the building schedule, and do the construction. I'm doing everything I like to do, including the door handles, the chairs, the tables, the lights. I design everything because nobody's stopping me.

OH

The running joke among architects is that it's always the interns who draw the door handles.

TD

Yes, but on the other hand, the door handle is the first interface with the building. And now I have the chance to control every detail. When I say, "Oh, I think we should have white leather on the table," they say, "Yes, yes. Great idea!" It's a dream scenario.

OH

Extraordinary! The buildings for Kvadrat are, from what I understand, in the nature of folded paper, paper hats, and paper plates. You started by taking the world as you find it in images and constructing sculptures out of paper. Now, you are actually creating spaces that have completely new purposes themselves. They will be inhabited, but their design reflects the quality of paper.

TD

I would say the logic of paper. Because you recognize certain features of the material itself, only on a larger scale.

OH

So, the sagging roof of SANAA is also a phenomenon of the logic of paper?

79

TD

Yeah. You know the notepads you can buy at Staples? The pages are a very beautiful color and translucent, and if you fold them in the middle and put them on the table, you have my roof, basically—

OH

It's a structural principle already!

TD

—sure, but more importantly, you have a translucent roof, like you do in a tent. I thought that would be quite beautiful to use for one of the pavilions because the translucency we talked about in the work of the Blaschkas is a wonderful quality. It's not like glass, which you see everywhere. Another part of the pavilion is the shape of a soda clerk hat. But I didn't want to use white because I'm not SANAA. I needed a color that was not associated with anything else. Not a primary color because that would be too corporate, and it shouldn't imitate a material that it's not, either. The shape sits in the middle of a green landscape where sometimes the sun shines beautifully, but very often there's an overcast sky. It has to stand out from that. I came up with a purple color, which I tested in about 800 different shades until I got the tone right.

I thought I would just be able to go to the store and pick a nice color but that didn't work at all. In retrospect, I don't know what I was looking for, but now we have a very, very distinctive purple-blue. It is a textile color, which gives the shape a much more fabric-like feel. I don't think anybody else is interested in that ... but that's cool with me.

Photograph of Louis Bierweiler, ca. 1935–1963.

Matthew and He
Petra Bla
Gold

Matthew Au and Mira Henry run the Los Angeles-based architectural design studio Current Interests. Matthew and Mira are both design faculty at Southern California Institute of Architecture (SCI-Arc) and have taught at Princeton University and the GSD.

Petra Blaisse's Gold Curtain is a space-dividing curtain designed in 2012 by Blaisse's studio Inside Outside for Piper Auditorium in the GSD's Gund Hall. The double-faced curtain serves as the backdrop for many public events and provides flexible spaces for uses at different scales within the large auditorium.

New Au
Mira
nry
ra,
se's
urtain

Klelia Siska

Detail of the black netting at the top of Inside Outside/Petra Blaisse's curtain in the Piper Auditorium at Gund Hall.

KLELIA SISKA

You often work with materials by layering them, almost hanging them on top of each other. This is really apparent in the *Silver House Studio*, where the exterior reads like a blanket or an oversized coat made of shingles and the interior a thick silver insulation blanket.[1] Where does this interest in layering materials come from?

MATTHEW AU

It's more reflective of an interest in the build-up of those layers, things that support and are equally supported by other things and yet retain a degree of autonomy. For example, with the shingles, we were interested in both the meticulous methods of their stacking—in the sense of color, form, and associations—as well as their supporting frames that are also stacked and hung on another set of frames. This interest developed early on in our collaboration, particularly through a set of photographs Mira took of the houses in her neighborhood. We became obsessed with what we saw as a gradual build-up and signaling of domestic facades through layers of hedges, awnings, stucco, window tinting, and curtains. The inhabitants cared for their homes in a way that created this layering of things.

MIRA HENRY

These ideas put pressure on the role of the architect. In nature, things change and gain layers and definition and thicknesses and identity and life. There's knowledge about how materials layer and about how things get ordered that exist not only in your education but also in your everyday life. As a mom of two, there are a lot of carpets and curtains and blankets in my life. There's a latent politics of the domestic present in the way I approach this work. Working in conversation and collaboration with Matthew, certain intimate and personal elements have developed into a practice.

[1] *Silver House Studio* (2019) is an in-progress design proposal by Current Interests for an artist's studio in Echo Park, Los Angeles.

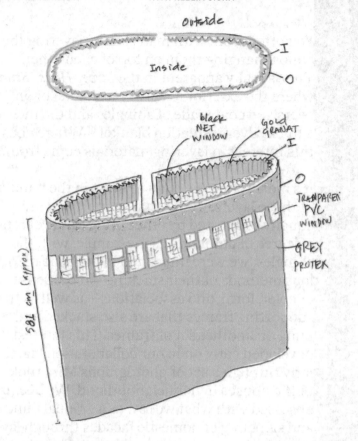

Sketch of the curtain in a loop, including notes on the material types.

KS

In the photographic series *Not White Walls*, you observed facade accessories like awnings and blinds in the vernacular domestic architecture of Los Angeles.® In the *Silver House Studio* project, you rethought the role of facade assembly details. I see you as historians who resurface and repurpose things. Is this close reading a way of questioning meaning?

MH

The way we formulate knowledge is through close reading and being very open about what that means. Close reading feels fundamental to the way that we create, understand, and synthesize things around us without necessarily turning these activities into architectural projects. The work doesn't have to wrap neatly into a super specific formal agenda; it can exist as a form of knowledge in the background.

® *Not White Walls* (2017) is a photography and installation project by Mira Henry that documents the vernacular architecture of single-story houses in South Los Angeles. The project highlights the personal identities of the homes' inhabitants through a series of building accessories such as windows, curtains, awnings, and blinds.

It's funny how it then turns into a set of assembly details, which is something less than a form. The process is more like, "This layer goes over that layer, and so it has to be heavy."

KS

Did Current Interests emerge from interests both in politics and in form? I'm thinking of how your work involves not just architecture but cultural projects as well. Are these what drew you together?

MA

In a way, yes. I've always imagined us as two sides of a complete project, something larger that could only be achieved through a shared conversation about architecture, art, and the world we observe.

MH

Two years prior to us forming Current Interests, Matthew gave a lecture at SCI-Arc about some work where the politics of material cost determined the form. And after that I went up to him, like, "I'm really interested in politics. But I'm a formalist, but I'm really interested in politics." He was like, "Me too." And I think that the politics side comes out of just being human, being in the world. With our backgrounds in art history and theory, we see politics and cultural projects as deeply intertwined, and we seek to define architecture in this way too. Why wouldn't there be a conversation that moved between social history and architecture, the political and the formal, artmaking and architecture? To our minds, those things just didn't seem very far away, and so we thought that we needed to make these conversations happen.

87

KS

I'd like to introduce our object, the Piper Auditorium curtain, designed by Inside Outside/Petra Blaisse. It is a two-layered curtain made of two different textiles: a heavy gray PVC fabric and a thinner gold polyester. I enjoyed finding many similarities in Petra Blaisse's sketches for the Piper Auditorium curtain and your own work, especially in the way that they emphasize assembly details as the core of a project.

MA

The first thing that caught our eye in the sketches is how they are hand-drawn, likely on the horizontal rather than upright, like a computer monitor. There is an angle to the page, as if a right-handed Petra Blaise is sketching out ideas while talking to somebody on her left. They're drawings made in conversation. And the curtain itself is also a form of conversation. We're enamored with the call-and-response dynamic between the two layers. One is this plastic,

industrial, vinyl-type material without a grain that wants to lay flat
and heavy. The other is this finer grain material that bunches and
shimmers gold. We like the idea of those being two separate things
that exist adjacent to each other, that move together but each in
its own way. We're obsessed with these sort of happy alignments
between things.

KS

Material behavior plays a big part in your work. How does the
specificity of the material become a reference for your design?

MA

I love that in her drawings Petra Blaisse lays out in exacting detail
every material specification and manufacturer ID number used
in the curtain. This is so familiar. We like to know every option for
the materials we work with—like every silver faux leather available

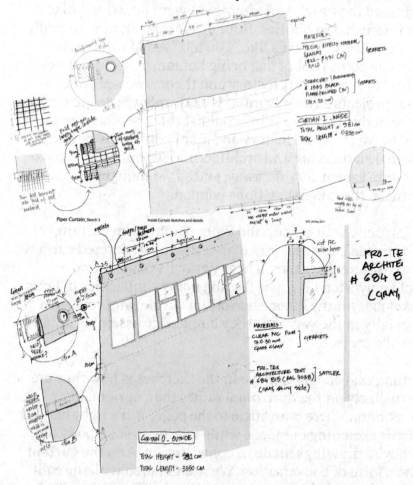

Sketches of the material specifications and assembly details of the Piper Auditorium curtains' gold and silver sides.

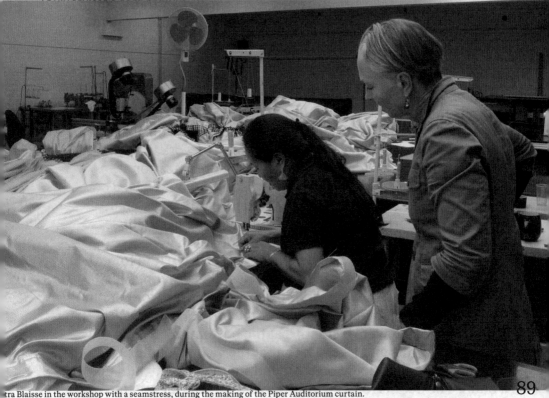

tra Blaisse in the workshop with a seamstress, during the making of the Piper Auditorium curtain.

—and understand how they behave, how they work, what their names are, where they're coming from. We love that the gold fabric from Gerriets is called Granat,[3] which is also the name of the last satellite sent into space before the dissolution of the Soviet Union.[4] An inspiration Mira and I often return to is the sewing laboratory at the JPL here in LA that produces the hot gold Mylar blankets that wrap around satellites and Mars rovers before they're launched into space.[5] We were always obsessed with the idea that there are these seamsters and seamstresses hand-sewing all of the covers to these things that exist beyond the limits of this planet. It seems so out of reach yet is so tied to the hand, to craft labor.

KS

I like that you bring up craft labor. There's this image of Petra Blaisse with the seamstress sewing the gold fabric. It makes you think how much the final product depends on a working hand and knowledge of material behavior. The gold fabric, for example,

[3] Gerriets GmbH is a German textile company founded in 1949 that specializes in stage design.

[4] The International Astrophysical Observatory, known as Granat, was a Soviet satellite spacecraft launched from the Baikonur Cosmodrome in the Soviet Republic of Kazakhstan on December 1, 1989. Granat was designed to observe energies between X-rays and gamma rays and operated for five years, outlasting the USSR. It stopped transmitting signals in 1998.

[5] Jet Propulsion Laboratory (JPL) is a federally funded research and development center managed by the California Institute of Technology for NASA.

was so light that it needed to be detailed in order to stand straight.
We see in one of the sketches that fishing weights did the trick.

MH

That's the kind of thing you never know until you're actually working with something at full scale. We're attracted to certain types
of materials that often resist rigidity or typical forms of drawing.
They become difficult to draw, difficult to understand until you
work with them at scale. That's interesting to us, to work with something that you have to attend to with different organizational
logics, measurements like "this to that" or "some amount based on
weight or affect" as compared to typical dimensioning systems ....
We like to find opportunities to use a material that needs a little
bit more orientation and understanding to work with it.

We recently fabricated and installed a room-size curtain for an
exhibition at the MAK Center in Los Angeles. The drawings of
Petra Blaisse's curtain in Piper Auditorium were at the front of our
minds when we developed the details for the project, particularly
the little weights that were fashioned at the bottom. We developed
the system of weights and levers such that the visitors could pull
on some small handles that would lift and squinch the curtain up
like a blind. The details for weighing down the material became
a performative and interactive moment.

MA

That curtain is also made with two layers. The exterior is a highly
reflective silver fabric, and the interior is a custom jacquard-woven
tapestry of a hedge that we designed. We've been working with
the imagery of landscapes and hedges for some time. The photos
of the work are funny because there are all these hands and bodies
pulling and pushing this hedge-curtain. It is like a real hedge,
with tangles of things caught up in it [*laughs*].

KS

So, let's talk about color. Petra Blaisse explained that gold was the
only option from the beginning because of the specific ambience
it can create with light and reflections. Your *Silver House Studio*
project contrasts a very dark exterior with a shiny silver interior.
Can you talk a little about your interest in color and how you make
your choices?

MH

Color is relational, it becomes interesting in relation with other
things. How deep is the color? How thick is it? These are the kinds
of questions we end up asking in the office. But what's amazing

about the silver of our curtain is that it's the exact opposite of how you described Petra Blaisse's gold curtain. We had a conversation with the photographer James Welling at the exhibition we did at Princeton, and he talked about how silver always resists photography, like it's this impossible thing to photograph.[6] We're really into this idea.

MA

We always return to these things that are difficult to document. Whether that's the color palette we're using or tones that are so dark and rich that they push the limits of a material's color. And this is the problem we had with documenting *Silver House Studio*: we took photographs of our addition against the silver backdrop of the house and then realized that all of our shingles were under- or overexposed and so lacked the subtlety of tones we spent weeks calibrating. Or, consider how the ink just rubbed off of the flyers we made for the project with Studio Lin. There's something about the these materials that we like, a fugitive nature, a resistance to being documented or fixed.

[6] The exhibition *Current Interests by Current Interests* displayed a series of mock-ups of the *Silver House Studio* in the North Gallery at the Princeton University School of Architecture in 2019.

91

FUNCTIONS

SCREEN + COLUMN   CONTINUOUS   MEETING OR CLOACK

LECTURE   ROUND TABLE   EXPO

...ches of the different functions of the space around the Piper Auditorium curtain.

KS

Inside Outside's website describes the curtain as a "party in a golden shell." When I first read this I couldn't help but think of your studio brief at the GSD. You asked your students to make a video about a party and think about "how bodies and garments in the space gesture, articulate, and collect light." I find this a beautiful connection between the studio and the curtain.

MA

We were actually looking at this photo of the Piper Auditorium curtain during the "Family Dinner" event and saying that it captured exactly our first ideas about the studio brief.[7] We were thinking of a space without any facades, a space that doesn't have to present itself out to the world, that it is fully internalized. And that was what they're doing in that picture of that event: they're turning the gold curtain inward and shutting out everything outside of it to make a space where they could produce a set of shared ideas free from external pressures. We love that.

In the studio we asked students to produce the idea of a party through video. This was an important format since it brought up the question of the tone and measure. I've always been interested in this idea of intonation, that you can completely change the meaning of a text simply by changing the way it is delivered. There's a video that I show my students, Martha Rosler's *Semiotics of the Kitchen*.[8] She goes through these various kitchen instruments— a knife, a pot, etc.—just naming them but also violently gesturing with each one. There's something about the information given through instruction, notated in drawings, or documented in a text that has always seemed incomplete until it is played or enacted. And this, for me, is what the video captures.

[7] *Family Dinner* was an event organized by the Harvard GSD student organization Queers in Design on April 9, 2019. Petra Blaisse's gold curtain was reconfigured as an enclosed room inside which a dinner-format discussion took place. The curtain's gray exterior was used as a projection surface on which the interior activity was shown.

[8] *Semiotics of the Kitchen* is a 1975 video and performance by Martha Rosler that parodies the image of the woman as a housewife in a kitchen. In the video, she moves around the kitchen, assigning one letter of the alphabet to every tool.

MH

That's right. With the video there's movement, sounds, lighting, gestures . . . a set of choreography and atmospherics that are at the origin of each project. Returning to the curtain, for instance, the curtain as a form is a powerful interlocutor for this work of articulating space. The curtain can be complete on its own as a foreground and a background. It has its own logic, its own beauty, and its own details. But there is also the way the air moves

...is presentation of GSD student Diandra Rendradjaja (MArch I '22), using the curtain as a room.

View outside curtain during "Family Dinner" event organized by Harvard GSD group Queers in Design, April 9, 2019.

around it, the way the light collects around it, the way bodies gather in relation to it. Those things are sensual and alive in nature. Particularly in our teaching, we're always searching for ways to pull those senses out, to create an alertness about the work. These minor things can become the objects of design. The thing that one designs isn't just the wall or just the floor detail, it's all these other things, this idea about a setting. And that's when the work becomes meaningful.

KS

Do you feel like the aspect of interiorization that "Family Dinner" played on reflects a gendered reading of interior/exterior conditions, which have been around since the 19th century?

MH

Sure, certainly. Although to be honest, I think so many aspects of architectural thought are entangled with gender and race. But to speak specifically about the technicality of curtains—it's funny because when I was working on *Rough Coat* in 2018 I was trying to figure out how to fabricate layers of material.[9] Matthew told me, "I think you need to sew it, Mira." And I was like, "I am not

w inside curtain during "Family Dinner" event organized by Harvard GSD group Queers in Design, April 9, 2019.

going to be the woman who sews." and he said, "But you are doing a blanket!" It just made sense, of course. My anxiety around sewing as a gendered construct was really entrenched.... That is why we need more voices, more people making architecture to subvert staid logics and to empower an expanded set of references and values. We wanted to do that with our studio and asked everyone to put their own identity and their own personhood into the mix. A party is an intimate thing. In the beginning, some felt uncomfortable with it, but they did amazing things. It wasn't always autobiographical. It wasn't one-to-one— like,"This is my identity."—but rather came out of a belief that close attention to social practices will lead us to overlooked regimes of thought.

KS

Petra Blaisse used the word "emancipated" to describe her curtains. She emphasized how these objects can operate independently of the architecture they're placed in. The curtains have their own life within the building.

⑨ *Rough Coat* was an installation Mira Henry produced for the SCI-Arc Gallery in 2018. The work is described as a facade-scale blanket, a panelized material system made of upholstery foam and flexible stucco.

MH

There's so much to say here about performance as a concept in architecture. On the one hand, curtains and associated soft systems in architecture entail some consideration of critical aspects of environmental performance. Acoustics, lighting, fireproofing, temperature control, etc., are brought to bear on these elements. Curtains, insulation, and upholstery are regulated, specified, and codified. On the other hand, these soft systems are deeply connected to spatial and social affects and practices. The curtain signals the drama that unfolds beyond. It is the tactile interface of the buildings we inhabit and maintain. While at times highly constructed, the curtain is often as simple and direct as putting a piece of cloth up in a window. Cloth, of course, can have deep, meaningfully complex histories as a product of industrial manufacturing and craft techniques. In this way, the curtain holds a middle ground—a mixed identity—between the informal and the architecturally regulated. Both, I would say, tend to be underconsidered in our discourse.

MA

Looking at the photographs of the curtain in Piper Auditorium, there's a moment right here in one image where it bunches up and looks like it's going over a chair. I love that moment: the curtain collides with the building. The PVC material buckles in a very different way than the polyester. The buckling is like buckling leather.

MH

I was thinking about behaviors. Like tolerance and certain more abject affects, the tired curtain, the curtain after the party. I think that we also look at materials when they are exhausted. It looks a little sad but it's beautiful. There is a moment when a little light buckle turns into a flop, and the material starts to look messy and a little shitty.

KS

Is imperfection then another one of your current interests?

MA

Imperfection often tracks with liveness.

MH

The fading of material on a model, the finger marks on a surface that are detectable only under certain lighting conditions— yes, these are things we talk about a lot!

gray PVC side of the curtain, partially folded.

AFTERWORD WITH PETRA BLAISSE

KLELIA SISKA

I spoke with Mohsen Mostafavi, and he explained how the GSD needed to have a good backdrop for public lectures. Did the school share a vision about the space with you?

PETRA BLAISSE

Mohsen called me and said, "We have this big auditorium, and it's actually impractical because we can't divide into in different areas. We also need a backdrop and more intimacy for lectures and presentations on the auditorium side

of the hall." So, the basic question was to make a flexible-division curtain to create two separate spaces if needed: one half being an auditorium with seats and a podium and the other a big open space for students to show their work. Instead of making a flat curtain that goes up and down or opens and closes, I thought it would be interesting to make a little room of it, so that you have a zone in between, perhaps for a small exhibition or a meeting, somewhere intimate to have

a conversation with someone. This acoustically works better too, because you have two layers of a double-layered curtain with an air chamber in between.

KS

Had you been to Piper Auditorium before?

PB

I went there with samples to consult with the technical staff if the materials we had in mind were maintenance-proof and if the colors and structures were right for the light there, which is very specific. You can't grasp it from a distance. We have daylight here at the office, and the Piper Auditorium is lit with a technical lighting system. It's always good to see patches of cloth or material samples in the actual situation of the site. What we also found out during the meeting was that the curtain needed to have an opening for projections from one side of the space to the other, for visual connection, as the technical room is to one side. The technicians should be able to look through to the other side. That opening became a copy of the actual windows of Gund Hall.

KS

The curtain is made of two opposite sides and materials. We're used to seeing its more festive gold side. But what about the gray side? When unfolded it can be totally straight, acting almost like a fifth wall for Piper Auditorium.

PB

The curtain was designed to have a very functional and a very festive side. The gray plastic is very "muscular" and practical—it's often used for covering trucks or boats. The material is very strong, can be cleaned with a cloth. It can also be used as a wall. You can put magnets on two sides that can hold things, so students can put up their sketches this way. Then, if you fold it open, you expose a golden, heavily pleated backdrop facing the auditorium. And if you pull the curtain further around, you create a backdrop of gray plastic closer to the auditorium seats, providing a more industrial working atmosphere, like in a factory. The golden backdrop can then face the other side of the space or be hidden inside the pulled out curtain, a complete loop.

KS

The other side moves completely differently. How important were the pleats for that reason?

PB

The inside is like a bonbon box: it looks really festive and very classic and catches the light.

And yes, this side is exaggeratedly pleated. The gold side is a bit kitsch, and the truck-plastic side has some kinkiness to it, especially because of the black netting we chose for the windows in the golden layer, like an enlarged net stocking. The window in the "truck" layer is made of transparent plastic. All in all, the windows look like those of the architecture itself. The movement of the two materials is totally different, as you say. One is stiff and the other is soft and full, more free to move. The entire curtain is pulled by hand, which I like, as it gives more freedom: you can park it anywhere and shape it as you wish. You can do any form or position, so you're totally free. If motorized, you always have to program the different positions beforehand, and you can't do anything else with it.

KS

How did you choose the gold color? I love the description of the project on your website, "party in a golden shell." Is this what you wanted to achieve? A party ambience?

PB

Well, yes. It was pretty obvious to us to create this golden interior. Harvard is a very elitist university, and on top of that everyone seems to be super intelligent. So, I thought maybe a bit sleazy, weird, kind of theatrical gold combined with a "workman" material could be a good thing. It's a bit over the top, but you can also consider it as chic versus functional. They're both not very expensive materials, but in combination with their scale they have a presence, and depending on their use, they change character.

KS

I wanted to show you the picture of the "Family Dinner" event, organized by the GSD student group Queers in Design in 2019. They used the curtain in a loop, made an intimate little room, and the light reflected beautifully.

PB

A dinner there! That looks fantastic. It's really used very well, huh?

Keller Easterling ○————————→ **Levittowns** ○——————
is an American architect, urbanist, are considered by many experts the
writer, and is the Enid Storm Dwyer formula for suburban housing develop-
Professor and Director of the Master ment in the United States during the
of Environmental Design program 1950s and 1960s. William Levitt was
at the Yale School of Architecture. an American real estate developer
Her writing covers global infrastruc- who envisioned these mass-produced
tures, economies, and policies that suburbs in New York, New Jersey,
shape space. Her recent books include Pennsylvania, and Puerto Rico, creat-
Medium Design: Knowing How To ing an unprecedented template that
Work on the World and *Extrastatecraft:* shaped the aesthetics and politics of
The Power of Infrastructure Space. postwar suburban life in the country.

ler
rling
owns

Kenismael Santiago-Pagán

KENISMAEL SANTIAGO-PAGÁN

What do you think Diane Arbus intended to capture here in this photograph of a living room in New York's Levittown?[①] To what extent is this image a marker of the disposition that developer Wiliam Levitt was trying to sell?

KELLER EASTERLING

The marketing of Levittown associated homeownership with patriotism. But if you turn down the volume of that rhetoric and just look at the organization, the disposition of Levitt & Sons is really its content. It was, as you know, an organization that was like a cross between a large-scale agricultural field and an assembly line. Things were done in multiples.

Levitt & Sons poured 17,000 concrete slabs, and framed 17,000 houses. Into these they shoved 17,000 TV sets, like the one in the picture. Residents ended up living in apartment-size dwellings that fit within the financial structure of the long-term, low-interest loan. So, it was not really so much a spatial organization as a financial one.

Suburbia started as a banking formula during the Depression to jump-start the economy. Through the Federal Housing Administration, so-called "merchant builders" like Levitt got blanket approvals for multiple homes. And that's why they look identical. Residents lived in a formulaic box. And I think you can see a little bit of that here in Diane Arbus's image, the perfunctory consumption of items designed to fit that box—the TV set, the couch, the Christmas tree, and so forth ....

KSP

In your book *Extrastatecraft*, you wrote, "The house was not [a] singularly crafted object, but a multiplier of activities. The developer, William Levitt, turned the site into an assembly line, and the homes into a population of commodities, from their frames and roofs to their TVs and washing machines." How successful do you think this model was as a multiplier?

KE

Well, I'd say it was extremely contagious. If that's the marker of success, it was successful as an agent of sprawl, as a way of retooling the land. It's still the reason for sprawl because new housing construction is still attached to the economy as an economic indicator and also associated

① Focusing on normalizing stigmas regarding disenfranchised communities and marginalized groups and working in and around New York City from the 1950s to the 1970s, American photographer Diane Arbus used her photographs to capture the raw reality of humanity. Her work transformed the art of photography by highlighting the importance of honest representation of all people, especially those who were usually not considered suitable photographic subjects.

103

ne Arbus, *Xmas tree in a living room in Levittown, L.I.*, 1962. Gelatin silver print, 14 ½ × 14 ¾ inches. Harvard Art Museums Archives.

with employment to measure the health of the economy. The construction industry that is part of that has not been retooled to provide employment in terms of deconstruction and reuse.

I think you can also see in the Arbus photograph that the industries were also tooled to supply materials for the house. The ceiling is eight feet tall because that's the way that the sheet goods like plywood or gypsum board were made. And so the Christmas tree has to be sort of cut off a little bit to fit within this low-ceilinged room. The whole world was calibrated according to the dimensions of the box, and every industry that made anything in the photograph—from the TV set to that lamp to the sofa to the clock—were marketing to that distributed consumer in place.

KSP

I'm really drawn to the notion of how the whole world is crafted or constrained to a Levittown box. In 1967, the sociologist Herbert J. Gans wrote in *The Levittowners* about what he called the "numerical cultural majority," the majority that produces a certain kind of Levittown demographic. To what extent is urbanization, although determined by planners, genuinely shaped by the sociopolitics that put pressure on this type of infrastructure, on the way we live and the way we dwell?

KE

There were all kinds of people designing ideas for the community. But the people that won and had the most impact were those who used the house as a banking, construction, and employment instrument. So, it wasn't the spatial arrangement that was important to them but the way in which it would jump-start those industries. These interests won the legislation, and the regional planners and Green Belt town planners lost.[②] Similarly, the automobile industry had the power to lobby to get an infrastructure built to sell their cars. And they got the public to pay for it. The car went hand-in-hand with this multiplier. There is a garage attached to each one of these boxes.

KSP

So in a way, the machine, the car, precedes what would become the way of living.

KE

Yeah, and there were many ideas about how to make interstate highways. There were lots of different plans, some for huge trunk lines that would go across the United States, and some that had more to do with the National Parks. Some were planned around the way people traveled between cities, and municipalities were powerful in getting money to drag highways through their cities. Some of that money allowed them to use highway construction for slum clearance and racial segregation and other big planning dreams.

② Used in land-use planning for retaining areas of underdeveloped agricultural land that usually surrounded metropolitan urban areas, Green Belt policies were focused on preventing urban sprawl by maintaining the openness of under- or undeveloped land.

KSP

Indeed, highways were used as a segregation mechanism just like these Levittown-type projects by creating zones that were tools to generate "multiple nested forms of sovereignty". Addressing how municipalities got money from this idea of creating zones made me think about sovereignty, and I want to touch on that a bit more.

KE

In *Extrastatecraft* I was looking at other multipliers outside our domestic sovereignty that were designed to produce free-zone enclaves in which global corporations can avoid taxes and environmental and labor regulations. Some of the corporations that were concocting these forms thought they would be temporary experi-

105

al view of Levittown, New York, ca. 1950s. Levittown Public Library.

ments to jump-start the economies of developing countries. And this takes us to Puerto Rico—

KSP

Exactly.

KE

—which was considered to be an island where rules do not apply. Some of the first of these experiments were in Puerto Rico and in the *maquiladoras* in Mexico, where factories were powered with cheaper labor. And corporations acted as if producing these abusive factory enclaves was a real act of benevolence.

KSP

A colonial "temporary experiment" that continues in the present. What would have become of us if it weren't for the benevolence of the United States, right?

KE

We are saying this tongue-in-cheek, obviously, but yes, American companies in Puerto Rico were saying, "We're bringing jobs and modern culture and technology and so on to this country that is lesser than our own. We're bringing people up out of poverty." That was their position. And there were also middlemen inside Puerto Rico who were building and promoting these factory enclaves as places where, "All you have to do is come and flick on the light switch. Everything else is going to be ready for you."

KSP

I find it so interesting how you mention Puerto Rico and local middlemen. Luis Muñoz Marín, who was governor of Puerto Rico at the time, is just one example. What does it mean to have the privilege or the audacity to create zones like this within Puerto Rico—a zone within a zone? What constitutes an unincorporated territory or, perhaps, a modern colony in the 21st century?③ And what does the colonization of Puerto Rico have to do with the desire to build, shape, and maintain this longing for the American city outside the American city, for the American suburb to be the American way of life? I wonder if, looking at the Arbus photo of Levittown, New York, and the photo of Levittown, Puerto Rico, we're even talking about the same American city or the actual American city versus the imagined, desired one that was experimented with as an economic project?④

③ In Downes v. Bidwell the United States Congress was granted complete plenary power over Puerto Rico. The decision established legal precedent designating Puerto Rico an unincorporated territory and subjected the island to the authority of Congress, which exposed the colony of Puerto Rico to diverse experiments, carried out by the US government. The Downes v. Bidwell decision was made in 1901, 62 years before Levittown, Puerto Rico, was built, which remains a model of housing development in Puerto Rico to this day.

④ Operation Bootstrap was a development policy implemented in Puerto Rico after World War II that rapidly industrialized the island's economy from agriculture to manufacturing and occurred in tandem with the formation of the Commonwealth of Puerto Rico during the term of Governor Luis Muñoz Marín.

KE

Well, these are really fascinating images, and I think the Levittown in Puerto Rico had something like 11,000 houses.

KSP

Correct.

KE

It's super interesting that the Cape Cod house became the model of suburban development in the United States because the Federal Housing Administration wouldn't approve modern houses with

vittown flag in Toa Baja, Puerto Rico, ca. 1963. Bettmann Archives.

flat roofs for fear that the design would bring the neighborhood down. Their sense was that in each neighborhood, the houses should look alike, that there shouldn't be multiple styles. That made suburban development more bankable. It was more like a form of currency in that way. The Cape Cod, early American style also went along with this kind of patriotic idea that was associated with Levittown. Some of the ads for Levittown were essentially saying, "If you buy a house in Levittown, you're continuing to fight for the United States."

KSP

It's impressive how many things you can come to know about a place just through an advertisement. The phrase "As Levitt goes, so goes the nation" is what journals and newspapers of the time used to describe the development, according to sociologist Chad M. Kimmel.[5]

⑤ According to the sociologist Chad M. Kimmel, the phrase "As Levitt goes, so goes the nation" was used in journals and newspapers of the time to describe suburban development.

KE

Some even said, "You're continuing to fight the war." I was really fascinated

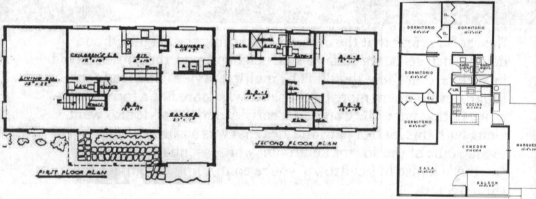

Levittown model comparison. New Jersey "Ranch" model and Puerto Rico "La Diadema" model.

when I saw these houses in Puerto Rico with flat roofs. Some of the Levitt houses had slightly modern details. They would have a little detail on the carport or something that looked modern. I don't know the history of how they decided on this kind of Miami-style with the cinder blocks. I've heard that having a cinder block house was something that Levitt & Sons promoted as a benefit.

KSP

There's a lot of oral history about why the houses in Levittown, Puerto Rico, looked like this. With Operation Bootstrap, the US government changed the whole notion of transforming a developing country into an industrialized country. They wanted to build houses that were strong enough to withstand hurricane-force winds but also modern and cost-efficient at the same time. Contractors had to perform some mental gymnastics to achieve this, but in the end, families ended up having a concrete matchbox with eight-foot-tall spaces. These boxes ended up being really hot all year round because of their flat roofs and concrete, which, as you know, absorbs heat. I guess they were thinking more about the economic factors rather than the quality of space.

There were about four models. Some of them were actually designed to be like a Spanish-Colonial revival model, although the Spaniards never built anything around the specific area of Levittown, Puerto Rico. They thought they were building something that would survive hurricanes, and the houses did survive until Hurricane Maria in 2017 and the unpredictabilities of a changing climate. We see now how these houses are struggling with massive flooding. Whenever there's a huge downpour, residents have to evacuate their home in kayaks or brave swimming. Otherwise, they're stuck until the water clears out.

KE

One of the things the New York and Puerto Rico Levittowns share, as I understand, is being built on swampland.

KSP

Yes, unfortunately.

KE

In one film advertisement for Levittown, I remember that the narrator said something like, "Here's the new development of Levittown on what was once only swampland." There was that sense of the swamp as something that you must quickly fill in, as if that constituted progress. The same sort of narrative accompanies this development. Swampland, obviously, is cheaper land. That was probably Levitt's calculation: he could fill in the swamp with earthmoving equipment, level it out, and eliminate the wetland. But obviously, it didn't work that way.

KSP

It's as if infrastructure didn't know boundaries. "We can put this wherever we want and however we want because we have the power to do so." I don't know if the ones in New Jersey and Pennsylvania experience the same flooding, but that's the aftermath. I think it's something that we can learn from, in terms of what type of infrastructure can be implemented where. One thing that strikes me the most is the infrastructure's role as a medium of expanding capitalist commodification and production over the beneficial qualities of a space. I think this is tied to the multiplier effect that you mentioned.

KE

Yes. I started thinking about spatial products by looking at these suburbs. But then we could look at many other kinds of repeatable, spatial formulas, from resorts and golf courses and cruise ships to whole cities like the free zones. There is a sense that land is not alive, that it is something that can simply be commodified. That land is property, a geometric and financial expression, and not a living thing. This attitude is so different from an understanding of what land really is—the crust of the earth. It is this notion of land as property that has accompanied our modern, Enlightenment thinking. Previously, land was often held in common, and there were many other forms of collectivity. But land has been commodified as property for these last few abusive centuries.

KSP

The land then ends up governed, controlled, and turned into zones, therefore enforcing the perception of land as something that can be conquered, exploited, bought, or sold. Is there any way to push back against that?

KE

Well, capital often utterly fails, in part because it is so lacking in information. Capital, with its tilted playing fields and thin abstractions, should not have power over the lumpier, spatial world of proximities and sequences and communities and the hard, solid things that we are supposed to know something about as architects.

I've been working on alternative land-holding organs. When capital fails, as it inevitably does, other kinds of community economies that have to do with mutualism and kinship can organize. Rather than thinking of one system replacing another, multiple modes of exchange might overwhelm some of the thin abstractions of capital with the heavy information on community and climate.

KSP

Do you think that places like Levittown produce new sociological relationships that require new, different types of governance and control? What could be an alternate reality?

KE

The forms we design are not just buildings but protocols of interplay. Some of the protocols of interplay that I've been thinking about are ways to put the development machine into reverse, to actually subtract or reverse engineer some of the more abusive forms of development. And Levittown is an interesting example of that case. Because of its multipliers, it doesn't make a lot of sense for an architect to go up to one of those houses and redesign it. That's not how you manage a field like that.

I do think that there is a kind of lingering disposition in the way something is organized, which means that organization has a propensity to still be the box that consumes more and more things. The Levittowns in the United States were a subject of interest because many tried to build onto themselves and build ways to make themselves unique. But it's very thin. It's kind of like wallpaper thinness or carpet thinness, or it was kind of signaling an expression of uniqueness or difference.

KSP

So far Puerto Rico ends up looking like a quasi-American suburb that is outside the continental United States. I keep thinking of

Aftermath of a flood in a Levittown house in Puerto Rico. Photograph by Denis M. Rivera Pichardo.

the notion of putting the machine in reverse. What do you think it would take to reverse the colonial experiment? How could we reverse many of the examples we've discussed, like the free zones as modern colonial tools? Puerto Rico's Legislative Assembly is currently moving forward with plans to establish the entire archipelago as a free zone with tax exemptions for very wealthy people that are willing to relocate to the island. How do we work to reverse that?

KE

It's extremely difficult to think about those changes. However, there are many things that might be identified as weak flanks, as openings. And again, it comes back to capital's failure, to its irrationality. In the case of the free zones, I've speculated about repositioning that wealth, quarantining that wealth, or relocating that foreign direct investment into existing towns, rather than into exurban enclaves. In terms of something like Levittown, I've speculated about what would happen if one looks at alternative landholding organs or ways to reverse engineer the sprawl of some of these developments when they encounter real danger like floods and hurricanes. One way may be to make mortgages—the very things that were the first contagion—contingent upon climate consequences rather than econometric consequences.

Then you might also allow a certain degree of collectivity so that mortgages could be grouped according to collective risk rather than as subprimes or bankable objects. They might even use their risk as a resource. So, if they, for instance, collectively sell very risky land back to the city, then their mortgages are rated incredibly high. The land that was not worth anything, that was completely underwater financially and physically could, in groups, have a completely different value because it could reduce collective risk for all. So, we could change the terms of that initial contagion to attach it to more tangible climate consequences rather than thin financial abstractions. It could then become a counter-contagion based on individual choices and the choices of municipalities.

KSP

Collective ownership. Based on community. On the people.

KE

Based on the community, yes.

Mack Scogin and Merrill Elam ⌐⟶ **(*nostalgia*)**
are the co-founders of their eponymous, Atlanta-based architecture
studio. Active in the professional and
pedagogical fields, they frequently
teach—often independently, sometimes together, and sometimes alongside architect and filmmaker Helen
Han. Their voices uniquely complement and contrast one another in multimedia studio courses such as those
they have jointly taught at the GSD.

is 1971 short film by Hollis Frampton
in which he burns a series of photographs on a hot plate. As each rapidly
immolates, a narrator describes the
content for the subsequent image,
pointing to the highly contextual relationship of sound and vision. This film
is part one of the *Hapax Logomena*
series and Parts I-VII are included in
the Harvard Film Archive.
"Favorite Things"
is a series of diptychs assembled
from Merrill Elam and Mack Scogin's
personal travel photography that
often accompany lectures as an unaddressed backdrop. The juxtapositions prompt viewers to reflect on
the unexpected similarities that emerge
between the renowned with the
seemingly mundane.

Elam,
cogin,
en Han

lgia.)
vorite
gs"

Linda Just

LINDA JUST

I had noncommittally pulled some videos from the Harvard Film Archive when I was initially preparing for a conversation with you, Merrill and Mack. Then, after realizing Helen's background in cinematography, it seemed like this great opportunity to have all of you in a dialogue about crossbenching, crossmodal experience, and the relevance of mixing media in practice. It made sense to use a series of Hollis Frampton's short films as a springboard, specifically his 1971 film *(nostalgia)*, given his avant-garde approach and strong interest in disjointed relationships between sound and image in cinema. There seemed to be some potential parallels with observations you've made within your own work, especially as it relates to the "language of difference" you described in one of your lectures at Boston Architectural College.

MACK SCOGIN

Whew, okay. We're ready.

LJ

There's a single line in the "About" section of your firm's website. And though it's short, it's profound. It explains that you're interested in going beyond mere problem-solving in architecture to design that addresses your curiosity surrounding the role of architecture in society. On the one hand, that says a lot, but on the other, it has some opacity, implying a deeper intention. So, I would be very interested to hear how you arrived at this approach and focus and how you started to work together with Helen.

HELEN HAN

Do either of you even remember? It's been ages!

MERRILL ELAM

We were introduced to Helen by Ted Paxton, her good friend and classmate from Emory University. She came to our office in the early 2000s, a few years after graduating, and we've been working together ever since in one way or another.② Helen then left us to go to the GSD, and we have criss-crossed over time.

① Merrill: Over the years, I have often had the privilege of sitting on the margins of Mack and Helen's studios at the GSD. When I step back and try to evaluate what they have brought to the pedagogy of the architecture design studio, I think of a quote from Joseph Cornell describing his files (who knows what wonderous things were in those files!):

> a diary journal repository laboratory, picture gallery, museum sanctuary, observatory, key . . . the core of a labyrinth, a clearinghouse for dreams and visions . . . childhood regained

I know of this quote only because Ed Eigen gifted us *Dime-Store Alchemy: The Art of Joseph Cornell* by Charles Simic. Cornell understood intuitively that the juxtaposition of unrelated disparate objects created new realities. Mack and Helen ask the students to observe, collect, play childish games, and make personal picture galleries. This is all to liberate the students to discover their individual cultural and creative selves, to get lost in a labyrinth of overlapping contradictions, and to make, in the end, architectural speculations that are original and fresh and beyond any presupposed capability or self-evaluation that might have been brought to the studio. These are studios as "a clearinghouse for dreams and visions," complex briefs that strive for unlearning and learning the world and the discipline of architecture anew. The Mack and Helen studios are ephemeral, they can only be experienced. The value of the exercise is measured through the lens of each student.

HH

Yeah. But one question I have is how are you defining the term "crossbenching"?

LJ

It's a term that Berlin-based practitioner Markus Miessen uses in reference to design work pursued with an outsider's fresh eyes and occasional antagonism, a practice of diving into territory that might be at first unfamiliar. That is perhaps a seemingly subtle difference between the traditional definition of "interdisciplinarianism," but it emphasizes the value of the initial uncertainty and friction between two disciplines at the moment when you hybridize.[3]

MS

In response to your definition of crossbenching, this is going to be a long story. Merrill and I were doing industrial projects early on at Heery, like warehouses and factories.[4] The more we did them, the more we ventured out into pushing ourselves and our design capabilities, and after a while, we got the attention of some firms like Herman Miller, Westinghouse, Becton Dickinson. They were industrial firms, but they were also interested in a certain kind of aspirational architecture and its influence on the spaces of the work environment.

Anyway, we started to attract those types of clients well into the latter part of the twenty years at Heery. We left in 1984 with the idea that we could leverage this background as a catalyst for our own work. We were very lucky that our first project was a satellite space for the High Museum of Art here in Atlanta. We had absolutely no experience in the project type, but we had done a significant amount of pro bono work at the High designing and constructing exhibitions for children's education in the arts.[5]

Long story, but our personal practice continues to take advantage of all those years of time- and cost-control experience

2 Merrill: Anyway, that's how we met Helen. For her interview, she came to the office early, and she caught me at the dishwasher. I said, "If you're going to work here, you have to be willing to do anything." Hence the dishwasher. [*laughs*] That was our first exchange as I recall. It was very glamorous.
Helen: It was the best meeting!

3 Linda: But I think it's a term that originates from the UK government, for those representatives speaking from independent parties. They sit on benches placed perpendicular to the majority parties in opposition.

4 Mack: Merrill and I were in school together at Georgia Tech. And we both worked for twenty years, or something like that, at a firm in Atlanta that was a bit of a renegade, Heery and Heery Architects and Engineers, later Heery International. Heery was not necessarily a renegade on the design side but more on the practical side. The firm was established around the idea that it was the architect's responsibility to control the time and cost of projects. That was actually really completely unheard of in the practice at that time. You did not do that.

5 Mack: But we didn't just design them. We built them ourselves. Hands on. It was a huge outlet for us to experiment. These were environmental and spatial exhibitions that tried to deal with the use of color, perspective, texture, materiality, all the elements of the arts, all sorts of different things incorporated into physical reality. It got us very excited about the art of architecture.

117

and the notion that aspirational architectures, regardless of typography or context, can be realized within seemingly irreconcilable constraints. It is these seemingly irreconcilable differences that sustain our explorations and liberate the architecture. You might say our practice is an exercise in crossbenching. In other words, we've not specialized in any project type, and every project that we do is a complete start-over. There's always initial uncertainty, always new

ing of diptychs from Mack Scogin and Merrill Elam's "Favorite Things" on the left and stills from Hollis Frampton's
talgia) on the right.

territory typologically and contextually. We bring very little from
any previous project, so we have no real "look" other than each project looking different, and so everything seems to be somewhat
of a one-off and a little weird because of that. It's almost because of
our lack of knowledge or our naivety, but we could not have done
our initial work without those years of practice background.

LJ

Seeing that charted out explains a familiarity and a technical rigor that one would assume from firms that tend to specialize: you apply that knowledge on a regular basis but branch into more customized sets of curiosities. It seems as though it was an evolution.

MS

Yes, but the customization is based on the context of the project type, and the place, and the aspirations of the client, not our own. What we bring is the capability or the interest in starting over each time with those givens as a new challenge. If you look at our work, it's very confusing to most people because there's no continuity to it other than the lack of continuity.[6]

LJ

Where does the interest in narratives and cinematic depiction come from? For example, I'm looking at some of the project descriptions for the World War II competition project in Gdańsk. You did a deep dive into metaphor and narrative, employing a very particular approach to architectural design, and that does seem evident elsewhere in your work, especially in your use of photography and collections of photography.

MS

Yes. I think actually the interest in the image and narrative came from our liberating experience at Heery. In this regard, as to our use of photography, it is our medium of choice for recording our own ever-expanding dictionary of narrative provocations. After all, the innate human instincts of intuition and talent continually evolve and are enriched through the initial and willful recognition of external sources. For us, all architecture embodies narrative. Or, more importantly, each architecture embodies its own aspirational narrative. As to our interest in the inherent cinematic narrative of architecture, it should be obvious that no architectural experience is realized through a single immovable image.

Although architecture is beholden to fixity, it is only understood through movement. Movement through space. So architecture has a reverse movie-like, cinematic aspect. While it is bound in fixity, it is also, by necessity, wonderfully and inextricably tied to motion. Our interest in film or moving images came from Helen, obviously, because she studied film. We can't make a film. What were you doing when you first came to work with us? You were still at Emory, right?

[6] Linda: I suppose the same things about continuity were said of Eero Saarinen. Design for its purpose, its place, its function.

HH

No, I joined the office about two years after graduation. My first project was to build a website, and nobody at the office knew how to do it. It was a great project because it immediately exposed me to the archives. I had to look through all the slides and figure out how to digitize them. Mack and Merrill have what they call the "Favorite Things" slideshow, which is phenomenal because it pairs images that they've taken throughout their travels. They have a very long history of their own interests in that medium, and so the transference to video was a natural progression in part because of the technological shift that made it readily available.

LJ

Do you find it odd to think of that reaction now, with the increased prevalence of architecture as a narrative device in film and the success of movies like *Columbus* and *Parasite*? Never mind that *Playtime* and *Stalker* had amazing architectural settings, and they have long had a major impact on many designers.

HH

The background of that connection was always there, with references to Michelangelo Antonioni and Jacques Tati. But those pivot around this idea of having a narrative script where architecture is a character or a supporting actor. The question is how does one talk about film within an architectural discourse where it needs to be more at the forefront. I think that is still something that is being explored and developed.

After the GSD, and the kind of catastrophe of responses that came from my thesis, [*laughs*] I basically convinced Mack to let me help with some of his teaching.⑦ It was funny because it started at first with just the option studio presentations. We were already exploring ways of conveying certain comments about architecture as a discipline at that time.⑧

⑦ Mack: Helen, she was a real outlaw at the GSD. She really threatened some people. She did a thesis based on film. It was just outrageous at the time, that you would actually use film in architecture and in design. Helen: I had looked through all the previous thesis videos that were available in the library, and they were always very animation-driven —show the building, do the walk-through, things like that. So anything that was outside of that norm . . . Either it's an architectural animation rendering that just describes the plan and section, or it's the extreme opposite, a beautiful abstract art film. My argument was that there could emerge something between those polarities. It never had to be an "either/or" scenario. Talking about architecture isn't solely dependent on a narrative script storyline, but it could position itself somewhere in between.

⑧ Mack: Over the years we did, I don't know how many of these compilation films for the option studios. You would not show probably 50 percent of these today, because they would not be acceptable for current audiences. We did one intro that was about kissing, and it was absolutely outrageous. It cut across multiple cultures. Helen: But we stopped the video right before they would actually kiss. Mack: Yeah. Saturday Night Live skits, movies, Marilyn Monroe, and who else? Helen: Once, we used a long continuous shot overlaid with contrasting music. That year, P. Diddy had come out with a new album, and we juxtaposed one of his songs with *Russian Ark*, which is a film that is entirely done with one continuous shot. And somehow, they coordinated together really well.

121

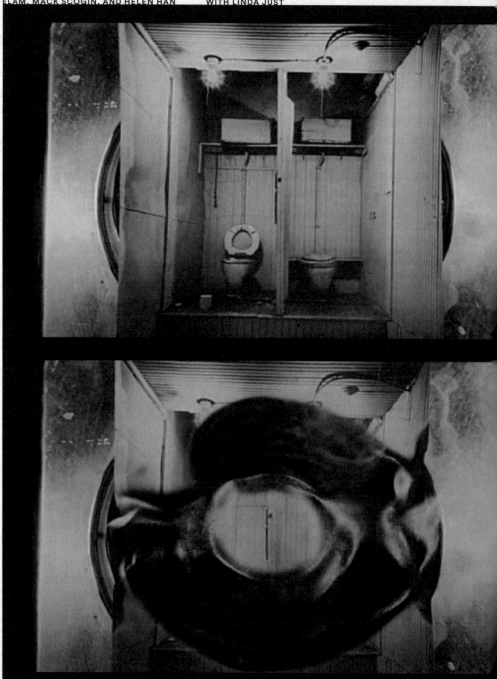

LJ
Do you have an intuition that they fit together, or is there something that you frame your curiosities around so that you can tinker until you hit the right thing? How is it that you know that these things give you what you need?

123

from Hollis Frampton's *(nostalgia)* on the left and a pairing of diptychs from Mack Scogin and Merrill Elam's "Favorite gs" on the right.

HH

Oh, we don't. We just test things out to see how they work. We don't have a preconceived idea of whether these things will work together. We just see how they pan out as we work with them.

MS

We've used film mainly in the studios at the GSD. We started requiring the students to do their own videos when it became a little bit more pervasive and everybody had the technology. It became very easy to incorporate video into the studio environment. But we use multiple media. The students write, they do videos, they play games, they, I don't know. What else do they do? Still photography, mapping, physical and digital modeling, sketching, drawing…

HH

Performance. We've had performances.

⑨ Helen: Oftentimes, they think that they have to understand how film works rather than make connections between these different platforms. You start talking about how film is really about sequencing. So, how do you start stitching together a beginning or an end? Or, do we even have a beginning? Could it be about a loop sequence? Or even just framing? How do you start taking components from your written narrative and really figure out the key elements you want to show in a different medium? I think those kinds of exercises start getting the students to understand architectural components that they had always thought about but never really knew how to express in their own work. Especially for spatial conditions that they were always intrigued by but never knew or had the tools or a mode of expression. So the exercises are a kind of freedom for them. In the back of their mind, they're like, "Oh, this is a different way of communicating abstract thoughts."

⑩ Linda: It seems as though being lost is a means of finding things you did not expect. I believe Rebecca Solnit wrote a book on this. A lot of what you're describing speaks to emotion and the sort of intangible collateral that comes out of architectural design. Is that something that you happened upon by accident or actively pursued through your exploration of different media?
Mack: It's something that we actually pursued, but I think that the extra media over the years has just opened up new and different ways for us to interpret and reinterpret aspirations around the architecture. We don't do it enough in our practice, quite frankly, but we really concentrate on it with the students.

LJ

What do you feel comes out of these cross-media experiments as a part of a process to push the work forward?

MS

We use them to cut across enough of these kinds of techniques for the students to identify themselves.

They learn more about what their real interests are in architecture through these different media. We do it to get in touch with them, to understand each student, but what really happens is they begin to understand themselves more and more. It becomes a very, very personal exploration for them.

HH

I think each student gains different components from the exercises that we throw at them. But it's always fascinating to see the kind of revelation that they get when all of the sudden, for example, they go through a writing exercise, edit it down, distill it to the components, look at it critically, and then translate it into a video format.⑨

LJ

It does seem as though there are many analogies for thinking through the progression of movement through space and programmatic schema.

HH

Right. But even in just a written piece, you have to make sure that all these components are there. Even if it's a nonlinear narrative, how do you pull together different scenes as a collection to provide an understanding of it?

Also, it's taking a stance that you don't necessarily have to explain every component to really get to the essence of a building or an architectural project.

LJ

That's an interesting way to phrase the process. I was thinking of the Frampton pieces as you were describing that. You have to really engage in imagination, and there's a cognitive dissonance between reading slides and picturing the scenes. It forces you into a position where you almost have to speculate on the image of every room by carrying for yourself a very particular, nuanced mental picture. That sort of strange, telescoping overlap seems like it would be a useful tool to have as you design, both to antici-pate your own personal impressions and also to empathize with other viewers and users.[10]

MS

We found that the students at the GSD have amazing backgrounds. 125
They're brilliant and talented beyond imagination. We do a series of game exercises to tap into that, and you just would not believe the energy.[11]

HH

But it's also surprisingly successful.

MS

And it's another medium. In the end, these exercises create a kind of passion for the studio that is shared. They understand that every-one's got a different project and different site. They're not in competition with each other. It just breaks down all kinds of barriers.

[11] Mack: The game exercises completely tear down all barriers that the students have, all the protective facades that they believe they need to survive at the GSD, and because they get prizes at the end of it . . . [laughs]
Helen: There are no prizes! There's no prize. [Merrill laughs]
Mack: It's so ridiculous. You would have to see the film of one of these game exercises to understand. They're incredibly creative, and they're brought to their knees [laughter], and they're yelling, and screaming, and running around. Anyway, it's really fun to see them let down their guard.

ME

It lets them critique each other in an open, productive discourse.

MS

This is not unreal stuff. I mean, if you're going to do good architecture, you have to have a great relationship with a great client. You've got to laugh with the client,

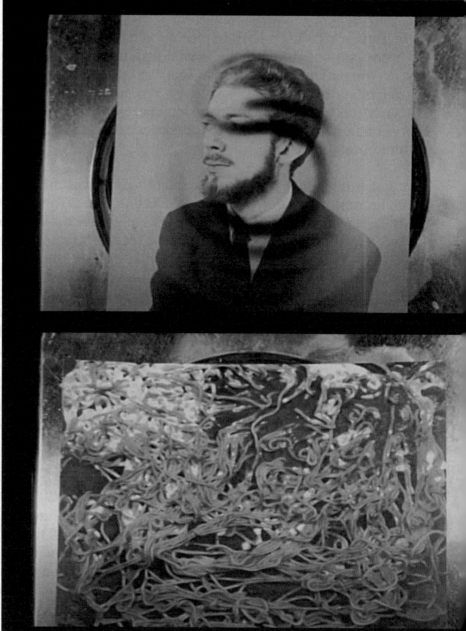

and you've got to understand their limits and the things that they
don't want but also understand the things that they never knew they
wanted. And that's what you want to give the client. Then, they
really love it.

So, with the students you are, in effect, simulating a kind of real-
life experience that parallels doing work for a really great client.
It does involve all these emotions and responses. It's as simple as that.

127

from Hollis Frampton's *(nostalgia)* on the left and a pairing of diptychs from Mack Scogin and Merrill Elam's "Favorite
gs" on the right.

LJ

But to your point, I think it probably takes time and effort to be
able to develop that rapport and ability to communicate and discover
a great client that you may not originally be familiar with.

MS

You need an arsenal to use that you can draw from, so these studio experiences are intended to begin the arsenal-building process.

LJ

When you developed this concept, was that your intention, to develop a different toolkit for communication, or was there something else?

HH

We knew that the students needed to come together quickly as a studio and be able to bond in a way that typical studios don't. But after the first few exercises, it was a surprise to see how each had to start figuring out ways to describe, for instance, a factory without saying the word factory. And all of a sudden, you remove all the architectural jargon.

It disappears from everybody's mind, and they resort to colloquial terms or redundant terms. I think that's actually a great way to start thinking about a project, to defer any background specificity that you had in the beginning and start from the essence of things.

LJ

It's interesting to hear you say it in those terms because it's almost a callback to the description that Mack gave about starting work on typologies that you weren't necessarily familiar with. Not directly, but in that you have to think constructively about what it is that you know and don't know and approach a problem creatively.[12]

ME

So what did you ask us to do here? Did we answer anything yet? We're just here rambling around.

LJ

To discuss the impacts of experience, of media, and their lasting presence in practice. I think that we've touched on that. But it's really interesting in that context to note how much of your own experience has melded into your pedagogical processes and the dynamics of your own practical relationships. It seems to also emphasize, too, the significance of per-

[12] Linda: There's also this connection between hypothetical scenarios and the reality of pragmatic processes. Mack: Well, Merrill has done crazier studios. One time she had the students find clients, but these clients could not be more than, what, five years old? Total bedlam, complete bedlam . . . The students brought their clients to the school, all these little kids. Anyway, it was ridiculous. Merrill: One of my students was a football player—he was actually on a football scholarship and studying architecture, which is almost unheard of. He was so funny with this little kid who was just dragging him around, outmaneuvering him. They had to have client meetings, of course. Linda: What prompted this idea? Merrill: [*laughs*] I don't know! Again, it's similar to what Helen and Mack do. It's trying to get the students out of their normative routine. I think it's like this new territory that you were talking about earlier with crossbenching. You get them outside of themselves, and I think that's the goo that holds these other disparate notions together. One little client said that his favorite secret color was white.

sonal relationships with space, which contrasts with how architecture is often presented in terms that tend to be far more third-person.

MS

Architecture should be kept contextualized. In the end, it's for people. It's for a particular client as well as a community.

HH

Related to this—I actually love the origin story of the "Favorite Things" slideshow. The thing that really got me was that instead of the typical "invite-whoever-to-present-their-work," Mack and Merrill actually would present a series of photographs that they just love, pairing them together as diptychs.®

LJ

So what are your favorite things to take pictures of?

ME

Well, anything that's of interest! We don't specialize in any particular quirky thing, but all things. What is interesting about education is you come out of architecture school having gathered up canonical and formal ideas. You've been exposed to architecture in a way that you haven't before, and then you go out the door of the school and you look at the world around you, and it's simply not anything like the Pantheon. You look around, and even those things that are very formal are all second-, third-, tenth- generation. So in a way, it's observational, about looking for something in your world that can inform architecture in a way that is new territory, this cross-benching. When I see a light pole coming up through a fruit stand, or a sign that doesn't make any sense or can be read three ways, I ask, "What are those relationships about?" I think one of your original interests is this idea about what is architecture's role in society. Society, in all ways, is manifested in this world around us . . . beyond the academy.

LJ

That's interesting because such image groupings are, it seems, about constructing new systems: collecting, the forming of vocabulary, and recontextualizing to create a syntax. You need to have the kit of parts first.

129

® Mack: Yeah. We would go to lectures and go thirty minutes without saying anything.
Helen: They would just flip through the carousel and show their slides.
Linda: Was that because you wanted people to form their own opinions, or was it just an easier process to kind of sit back and absorb?
Mack: We're terrible at presenting anything. What we do love to do is pair slides and share what we enjoy seeing. So, this was a fail-safe way to distinguish ourselves.
Linda: But it sounds like you did it a few times, so clearly there was some success to it.
Mack: We did it a lot of times. We had a contest with Frank Gehry to outdo his number of slides to show, and we beat him out easily because all he would show was his projects. We like to think he was very jealous, by the way.

HH

Right—yet not presuming what that would be before doing it.

LJ

Thank you so much for your candor and insight. I was promised that it would be an entertaining conversation, and I'm not disappointed.

ng of diptychs from Mack Scogin and Merrill Elam's "Favorite Things" on the left and stills from
s Frampton's *(nostalgia)* on the right.

MS

Don't repeat anything we said.

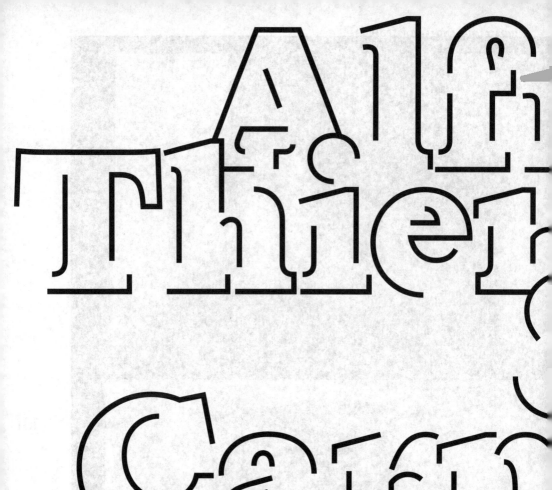

Alfredo Thiermann ⌁⟶ is an architect and cofounder of the firm Thiermann Cruz Arquitectos in Santiago de Chile. He is an assistant professor at the École polytechnique fédérale in Lausanne, Switzerland, and was a design critic at the GSD. His research centers on architecture's generative engagement with other disciplines, namely sound and film.

The Carpenter Center ramp ⌁⟶ is a pedestrian ramp serving as the organizational axis of the Carpenter Center for the Visual Arts. At its entrance from Harvard Yard, the ramp expresses the original Le Corbusier design, but its termination on Prescott Street is the product of several collaborations over time. It is the only building designed by Le Corbusier in North America.

redo
mann
enter'
ter'
mp

Julia Spackman

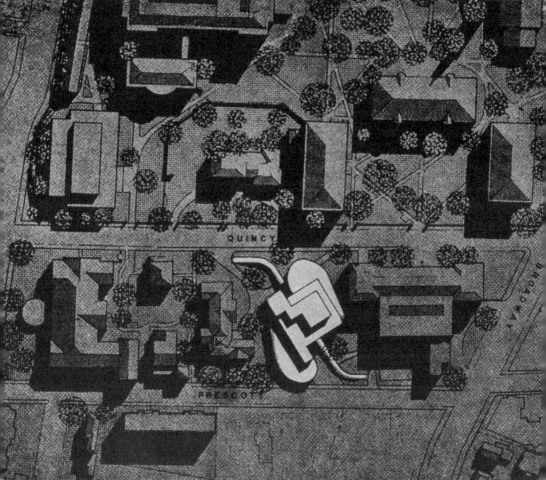

Site plan of the Carpenter Center ramp showing its connections on Quincy Street, to the west, and Prescott Street, to the east.

ALFREDO THIERMANN

Have you been looking at the Carpenter Center a bit? Do you find the building interesting?

JULIA SPACKMAN

Yes, but the building less so than the ramp, if the two can be separated. I visited it often over the past two years as it was the only quasi-interior space at Harvard that could be accessed during the pandemic. I was interested to learn that the empty space I encountered is only one of many iterations. We're standing at the base of the original ramp, and at the end is its third revision, by Renzo Piano Building Workshop as part of their expansion of the Harvard Art Museums. But between this latest iteration and the original was a second translation by Gwathmey Siegel Kaufman Architects for the Fine Arts Library addition to the Fogg Museum. These design iterations are interesting in and of themselves, but the way the form is recontextualized by subsequent designers denies Le Corbusier the single authorship we often assume.

AT

Originally the ramp was supposed to go all the way up to the roof, right?

JS

Another internal ramp was designed to continue the ramped circulation to the roof, yes. The coordination of this project fills an entire chapter in Eduard Sekler's 1978 book *Le Corbusier at Work: The Genesis of the Carpenter Center for the Visual Arts*. It describes pretty vividly how Guillermo Jullian de la Fuente worked through the Carpenter Center's plans. He determined that the freight elevator and the internal ramp could not coexist, and that was the end of it.

AT

Jullian was in charge of the project at the atelier. He was Chilean, and I thought you may have chosen me because of that. It's a very Guillermo Jullian project.

JS

In what ways?

AT

He was a very formally gifted architect. In my mind, he did slightly weirder projects, but the Carpenter Center belongs to the genealogy of Le Corbusier projects in which Jullian was involved, like the Venice Hospital, for example.

135

JS

It's weird even within his larger body of work?

AT

Formally it's more eclectic. It's less of a one-liner, less diagrammatic. It responds more to site conditions. I mean, that's my interpretation, because I've known Guillermo Jullian's work since very early on in school. We were shown his drawings—very eclectic. The Carpenter Center resonates with some of these works on a more visceral level.

JS

The building seems like a combination of one-liners. In the Sekler book, Jullian quotes Le Corbusier as saying that since the Carpenter Center is his only American building, it should contain all of his architectural elements.

AT

Yes, you also perceive fragments of other projects. For instance, this corner here looks like the little Tower of Shadows that was built in front of the big Palace of Assembly in Chandigarh, which was almost like a study model, but here it's a part of a building.

JS

I love the animation of the blank faces with the trees. But let's begin our way up the ramp.

AT

Let's go. Speaking of collaboration: one or two weeks ago, I came here with my friend Dominga Sotomayor, a very good filmmaker with whom I recently did *Turba Tol Hol-Hol Tol*, the exhibition at the Chilean Pavilion for the Venice Biennale. She teaches here. We came and stood on the ramp with Jean-Louis Cohen, and Dominga took a beautiful photo. And then, Jean-Louis told us all about this building.

JS

And you know Dominga from your work for the Biennale?

AT

I was invited by the Chilean curator Camila Marambio to think about a project that could materialize her research on the peat bogs of Tierra del Fuego. She wanted to work with a filmmaker, a sound artist, and an architect and build from that constellation. She decided on the sound artist Ariel Bustamante, Dominga, and me. We began

View of the Carpenter Center ramp from Prescott Street.

our collaboration by considering
a format that could visualize a landscape that is almost invisible. For all
of their cultural and ecological relevance, the peat bogs have no imaginary, not just in Chilean culture
but in general. So, what is the right
format for this? We started looking
critically at the history of panoramas
and dioramas, specifically noting
how nature has been represented
and made to travel to international
exhibitions and how problematic
those formats have been. We established a critical relationship with
that genealogy and came up with
something a little different.

JS

A diorama showing something
below the earth? Oh, look how the
score lines continue as cracks.

AT

Harvard President Nathan Pusey, Alfred St. Vrain Carpenter,
Helen Bundy Carpenter, Harvard GSD Dean Josep Lluis Sert,
and Mrs. Sert, May 27, 1963.

137

It became a material pursuit. We worked with the actual vegetation
that covers the peat bog, *sphagnum* mosses, and created a bioplastic
screen made of algae. The images projected on the screen were
fuzzy, and sometimes you could see through the screen, into the real
nature. In this way, you were both inside and outside the diorama,
traveling into the depth of the peat. Of course, the sound component
was very important for Ariel's content as well as its physical placement. Sometimes we were inside the sound, and at others it seemed
to come from afar. That involved the three of us, but the group
behind the project was much larger: scientists collaborated with us
and also the Indigenous poet Hema'ny Molina, who belongs to the
Selk'nam culture, the original inhabitants of Tierra del Fuego. At the
end we were a very big group, like a crash course in collaboration.

JS

Was there any hierarchy in this? Were you following anything more
than the curator's intention?

AT

Well, the curator selected us "artists." We three had more agency
in decision-making and a head start determining the format. Bigger

lines were defined as other people joined. But also, for example, the environmental conservationist and ecologist Bárbara Saavedra joined the project way before us—she's been working on conservation in Tierra del Fuego for decades. So, there was some hierarchy, which I think is actually very important to get anything done.

JS

Hierarchy and deadlines, yes. Let's pause here for a bit at the top of the ramp.

AT

Ariel had been working a lot in Indigenous communities by that point. He said that by the time we started working, a certain degree of hierarchy and decision-making was almost already naturally established through the different skills of our collaborators. It wasn't imposed but it emerged.

JS

Could that emergence be designed or specifically encouraged, or is it a natural product of bringing together well-intentioned, open-minded collaborators?

AT

You need a disposition for collaboration, I think. Otherwise, it doesn't fly. Difference of expertise also matters because then there's respect for otherness rather than overlap. So, in a way, difference does matter, but then there are problems.

JS

A problem in that supposed utopian situation? Are you fine up here? The wind is quite strong.

AT

Oh, yes. I mean, it's not our problem so much as it is an inevitable difficulty. Sometimes there are inherent contradictions, and it is sometimes difficult to make simple decisions and reach consensus. It's all part of the process, but it's a very different way of working. Maybe not for me, because my practice of a decade or so doesn't have a proper office structure. Everything I've done is through collaboration and always with people of different expertise. The filmmakers engage in a hugely collaborative endeavor but of a different model that doesn't exactly map onto architecture. Their way of working is more hierarchical and structured; people know their roles and the limits of those roles very well.

JS

Though our infinite digital platforms purport collaboration, there's nothing like sharing physical space. How did that collaborative decision making occur digitally? Did you share partial mockups?

AT

There was a lot of digital work, but what saved the project, I think, was that 20 of us traveled together to Tierra del Fuego for 10 days. We met there from all over the world. We did a series of activities, rituals, practices, excursions.

JS

Rituals? At what point in the process was this?

AT

Let's say halfway through. We knew our intentions and somehow tested them in Tierra del Fuego in order to change them. It was the right moment for it to happen.

JS

I'm getting cold, let's continue down.

AT

The project was all glimpses and translations from medium to medium until it reached its actual physicality. For example, we used a screen from the Department of Geology here at Harvard that was only one third of a circle.[1] Ariel composed the sound based on these fragments. There were a lot of digital exchanges and drawings, and all were approximations until the last moment of install, when it miraculously worked.

139

JS

What was the intention behind the project's credits? The long list of collaborators seems to preclude any individual egos.

AT

There's this contemporary trend in which one person capitalizes on a project involving even a hundred collaborators. In Spanish we call this *ley ovejuna,* "sheep's law." We chose to not engage in such a practice because of the project's political message. But we still live in a culture that Ernst Gombrich defined as "idols and not ideals," where a forum is more often given to specific people than to specific ideas.[2] Certain actors, by virtue of their cultural production, get a forum to broadcast the message of their given project. In our case, we chose to amplify one another.

JS

[1] The screen came from the Visuali-zation Research and Teaching Lab directed by Rus Gant at the Harvard Geological Museum.

[2] Ernst Gombrich, "Myth and Reality in the German Wartime Broadcast," lecture, King's College London, 1970.

In that answer, though, I still hear tension between the individual and the collective. Ah, and beneath us 1963 meets 2014 as the grate marks the transition between Le Corbusier's ramp and Renzo Piano's.

AT

It's a very delicate balance between leveraging the figure of the singular author and not diminishing the amplification power of all the voices involved. We all have different forums in which we can speak, disciplinary or otherwise. The project amplifies those different voices instead of canceling them.

JS

In amplifying that multitude, did you ever encounter disagreement among your collaborators' interpretations of the project?

AT

That's the thing: you create work, and then it acquires a presence beyond your reach. One person might have one interpretation; another person might have another. I think this is one of the values of art. More relevant for us is the impact that this kind of collaboration can have in Chile's current political situation. We're writing a new constitution that legislates over nature and Indigenous people—

JS

—women's bodily autonomy—

AT

—yes, that too. So, the politics of our work is extremely timely and will hopefully impact the debates that are happening in Chile.

JS

If you value all interpretations of the work, especially in this political setting, is there any merit in explaining the work at all? Or is it meant to be a truth perceived sensorially?

Werner Otto Hall addition to the Fogg Museum extending the ramp, Gwathmey Siegel Kaufman Architects, 1991. Demolished in 2008.

AT

People approach the work with different layers of context. If you confront it knowing nothing, you still get a big chunk of meaning from the aesthetics. Then, if you read the exhibition text on the wall, you form another relationship with the work. We do guided tours and have the archival website to add even more layers. There's merit in explanation, knowing that the best efforts will absolutely fall short of totality. On the other hand, a work should describe itself through a direct relationship. If it doesn't work like this, then the work is a bit of a failure.

JS

So, the project involved multidisciplinary collaborators with their own diverse backgrounds and contexts, but how could you prepare the work for an even more inclusive audience? Was radical acceptance and engagement an intention as it entered the world physically?

AT

Conceptual accessibility was important to us. At the beginning, I had many exchanges with Camila about the format. For instance, is it an actual screen that you sit in front of? Then, I became relatively convinced that it had to critically deal with the genealogy of panoramas, which engaged an early form of popular culture. When we first spoke with Dominga about a circular projection, we didn't have any visual expectations or precise references. Instead of giving a super sophisticated one, she brought up the popular film *Arrival*. In that film, and with our project, there was a political intention to speak quite directly to a broader audience. It's very layered. Some

141

Museum renovation and expansion extending the ramp, Renzo Piano Building Workshop, 2014.

aspects require a deeper involvement with the work. It captures people's attention to encourage further engagement with these processes and go beyond the venue of the Biennale itself.

JS

It does. Shall we head back to Gund?

AT

We went full circle. This is a great idea for an interview, outside and walking a bit.

East–west section drawing of the Carpenter Center for the Visual Arts by Le Corbusier.

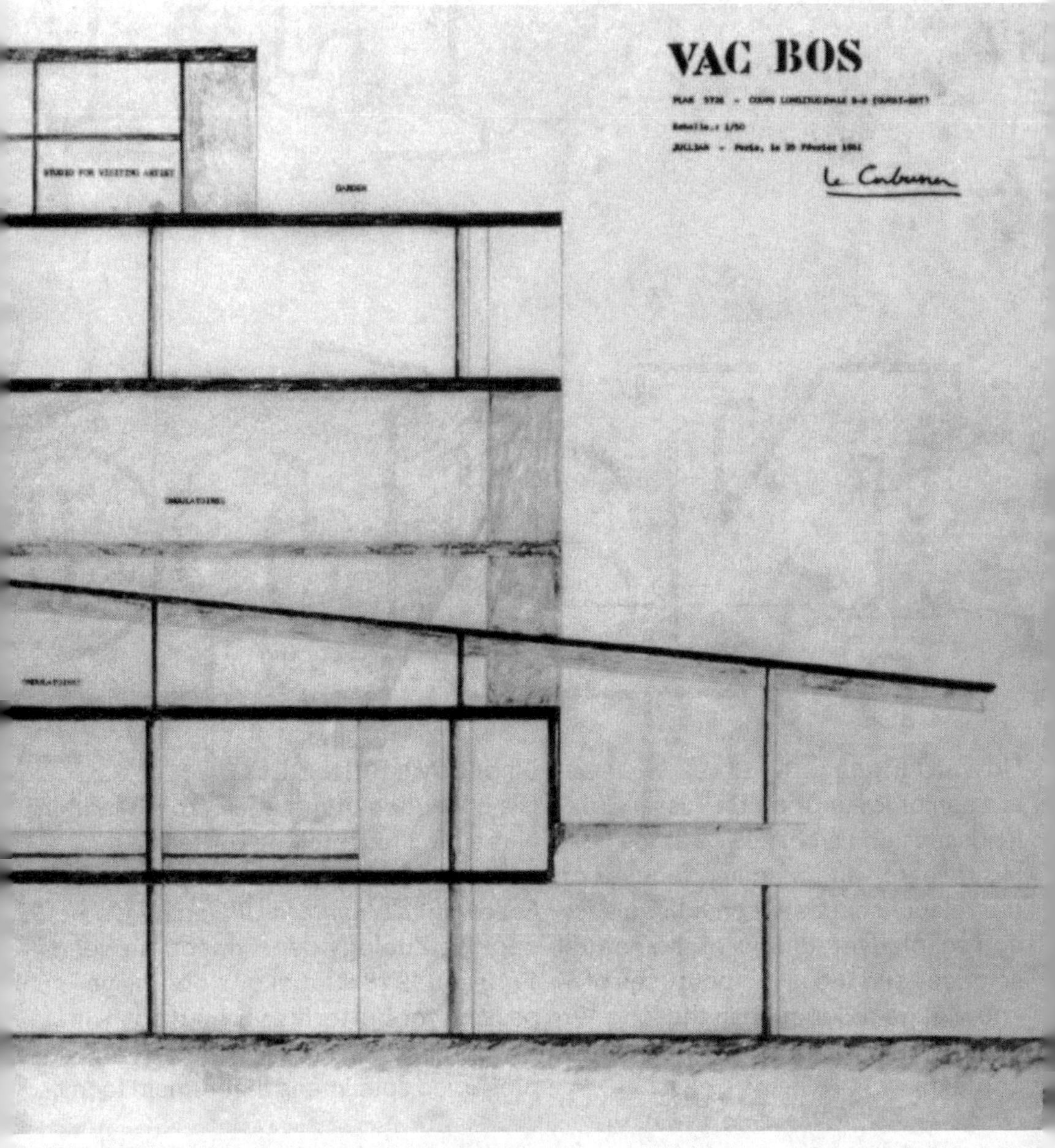
VAC BOS
STUDIO FOR VISITING ARTIST
GARDEN

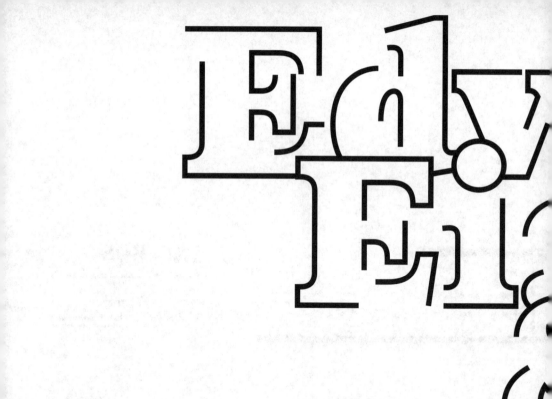

Edward Eigen ⌐────────────→ **Nabokov's Butterflies** ⌐──────

is a senior lecturer on the history of
landscape and architecture at the GSD.
His research and teaching focuses on
the relationship between humanistic
and scholarly traditions of the natural
sciences and the allied practices of
knowledge production in the long 19th
century European and Anglo-American
contexts.

is a collection of materials from Vladimir
Nabokov's research on butterflies
including during his time as a Research
Fellow in the Harvard University Comparative Zoology department between
1942 and 1948. Nabokov's obsessive
passion for butterflies is on display in
the documents, notes, sketches, and
preserved specimens that remain today.

ard

en

kov's

flies

→Elif Erez and Emily Hsee

EMILY HSEE

Many know Vladimir Nabokov for his novel *Lolita*, but he was also a highly respected lepidopterist. He studied butterflies. We've prepared a few images on a slide deck and want to share this map.[①]

Illustration depicting a map of the three-week, cross-country road trip Nabokov took in 1941. Georeferenced by Suzanne Rab Green, a zoologist and curatorial assistant for the American Museum of Natural History.

ELIF EREZ

Nabokov started volunteering at the Museum of Natural History in New York after he moved to the United States. In the museum's archives, a scientist found a box of butterfly specimens that Nabokov donated, all within the year of 1941, from different towns across the country. The scientist then georeferenced them by date and location, which led her to map out a road trip that Nabokov took in 1941. A lot of the roadside motels and scenery that Nabokov saw on this trip inspired his novels, including some scenes in *Lolita*. These specimens were a loose collection of cards that, when laid out on a map, allowed the scientist to surface a narrative about a road trip we now know influenced other fictional narratives.

① Ed: When I grew up, we referred to a presentation as a slide carousel or slideshow because that was the technology, and the carousel was, quite literally, circular. There was kind of an economy and a mechanism involved, whereas it's interesting to me that your generation refers to a presentation as a deck, which I assume refers to PowerPoint or some kind of stacked presentation on the screen. This might actually relate to Nabokov's use of index cards to organize his thinking and also his classificatory work.

EDWARD EIGEN

Oh, that's beautiful for a number of reasons, including the respect for the practice of conducting field research in natural history and taking notes on the place in which a specimen was taken. That place where a species thrives figures into the diagnosis or the specific description. I'm thinking of the binomial *Fragaria virginiana*,[2] for example, where the place-name Virginia forms the specific epithet. The place often finds its way into the name.

I was also going to say that so much of Nabokov's quasi-professional thinking about evolution had to do with allopatry, which is when isolation causes separated populations of a species to develop divergently. The geographical dimension matters greatly to this process.

This project of cross-referencing is also absolutely beautiful in the way in which it creates narrative by another means. *Lolita* has one of the most beautiful road trip scenes in American literature. That highway America with neon signs and road stops is quite vivid. It's been many years since I read the book, but it's one of the earlier books I read, so it was constituent in shaping my internal literary imagination. Needless to say, my view of the book has evolved, especially since reading Julia May Jonas's novel *Vladimir* from earlier this year.[3] Anyway, this is a lovely diagram.

EH

In her *New Yorker* piece, "Vladimir Nabokov, Butterfly Illustrator," Elif Batuman writes, "Over time, Nabokov's fixation on morphology and taxonomy—form and classification—shifted to, or perhaps turned out to have been all along, a fixation on history. He began, in the editors' words, 'imagining spatial variety as if it were temporal development,' assembling narratives, mapping the course of change over species and over geography." There's a multiplicity of beautiful intersections in his work. There are crossovers, not only between his literary work and lepidopterist work but also between geographical and temporal dimensions.

ED

Emily, that makes me think about the issue of classification. I think students have this sense of classification as a static representation of things in the world, that there are these categories, or boxes, or kinds, or types, or even species, family, order, or genera that are unchanging. We've divided things up. That's how they are. That's how they were named. That's how they've been. I think a lot of students lose sight of the fact that any classification is, in fact, a derived state of things. It's bound to changing desires for order, which is itself an unfixed state or quantity.

Nabakov pursued an evolutionary or phylogenetic process. He started off as a traditionalist looking to divvy up nature,

[2] *Fragaria virginiana* is the scientific name for the Virginia strawberry, wild strawberry, common strawberry, or mountain strawberry.

[3] *Vladimir*, a 2022 debut novel by Julia May Jonas, deals with sexual power and politics on a college campus. The gestures of its title, cover, and plot nod to Nabokov's 1955 novel, *Lolita*.

as it were, and then realized that the salient morphological features of these butterflies he was looking at were the result, consequence, or manifestation of profound historical modifications. He is, exactly as you said, looking into time. His ordering principle is dictated by a space-and-time relationship.

When I was in grad school studying biological and botanical systematics, I hatched this crude analogy between a grocery store and classificatory thinking. Go into a large grocery store and simply notice how things are arranged. Dairy items are placed together, and so are meat items, and so are vegetables and fruits. Some things

An array of detailed wing-pattern drawings on cards by Nabakov combined for simultaneous comparison.

are arranged according to temperature or the need to be misted. And then certain things are arranged by use. For example, nuts are not in the aisle that might be determined by botanical nuts or seeds or fruits but rather in the aisle with baking supplies.

I batted this idea around for a while with a teacher who I'm very fond of. He said to me, "That's all fine, Ed, but that's just where the classification is now. The real question is how those things were arranged 10, 50, 100 years ago."

It's not just about what the classifications would have looked like 100 years ago, it's also about what the organism would've looked like 10 or 20,000 years ago. Classifications constantly shift, and Nabokov is asking us for an understanding of them that considers space and time. I try to make students aware of that, but I know they want to understand classification as a lever for confronting certain regimes of power that are calcified, if you will, maybe reified, or even lithified in these classificatory schemes. But the schemes themselves change. The things they're meant to describe are products of change because we have, like all other organisms and like grocery stores, evolved over time.

EE

My high school biology teacher used to say, "People like putting things into boxes."

ED

There's certainly something to be said for the boxes we use. As Nabokov's investigations in lepidoptery advanced and, in particular, as he started using microscopes, he identified the genital organs as one of the most reliable features for thinking through speciation. Nabokov gave some of his butterfly specimens to the Museum of Comparative Zoology, which now holds a "sacred" collection of butterfly genitalia. There you have this collection of these dismembered parts. They have their own boxes.

149

The instrumentality of natural history is a terribly interesting issue. One of the things I read leading up to this discussion was the article "Butterflies" that Nabokov wrote for The *New Yorker* in 1948. There's a picture of him as a field naturalist. He has a small wax paper envelope that he's about to put his specimen in. This image already invites this beautiful layering of materiality, of the diaphanous wings of the butterfly and then the wax paper, which itself has layers of folds. There are all of these lovely, quite literal visual references and implications of meaning. He's also holding a little tin bandage box, which I love because the strips that are meant to tend to wounds have been used up, presumably because he got little thorns and bristles on his knees and ankles when he was in the field.④

④ Ed: The tin box is so typical of the naturalist. If you botanize, you use something called the vasculum to keep specimens that you collect in the field. One of Linnaeus's students, who was named Solander, invented another kind of box that was used to convey specimens back from places that were far from the metropole. And there are Wardian boxes, which were kind of like mini glasshouses, that were put on ships to convey specimens.

The point, Elif, is that the material culture of that box is beautiful and varied, and it scales up from the envelope to the box in which the envelope is kept, to the box in which the boxes are kept in the museum, and then to all the publications and forms of media that come out of it.

EH

It's funny that in the digital age we still organize our thoughts and information in a file inside a folder, inside a folder, inside a folder.

ED

Absolutely.

EH

On the topic of knowledge and information collecting, I want to share a quote from Nabokov's memoir, *Speak, Memory*: "I cannot separate the aesthetic pleasure of seeing a butterfly and the scientific pleasure of knowing what it is." This makes me think about the allure of the butterfly, specifically, including its place as a bridge between the sciences and humanities, the mysteriousness of its metamorphosis, and the ways in which it is very present in mainstream culture in a way that other bugs or insects aren't, like in *Alice in Wonderland* or *The Very Hungry Caterpillar*. I'm curious about your thoughts on the fascination with butterflies and also on the overlap between aesthetic fascination and scientific pleasure, as Nabakov calls it.

ED

I read somewhere that Nabokov had synesthesia, the condition where you read the number five and you sense a color, like red. It's this fascinating, unbidden overlap of sensations. He was seeing, sensing, hearing, feeling, tasting the world all at once. Nabokov's writing has a preternatural ability to evoke sense upon sense, amounting to a thickness of experience. It's just so rich. Nabokov's statement, "I cannot separate the aesthetic pleasure of seeing a butterfly and the scientific pleasure of knowing what it is," is anything but naive. As a narrative about modern scientific knowledge, it's one of unveiling, mastering, exposing, laying bare, demystifying, and even measuring, quantifying, and verifying. It's about the pleasure of knowing. It's this kind of inversion of power, a redirection of desire.

In "Butterflies" Nabokov talks about his childhood. It's very tender. It's very lovely. He grew up in this fantastically privileged world, which was then lost. But it is in the countryside at Vyra, the family estate, where he does his first gathering of insects. He narrates this alongside a very tender portrait of motherly love. His mother is his ally and his accomplice in his first lepidopteral studies.

At one point, he describes his anticipation. He experienced a kind

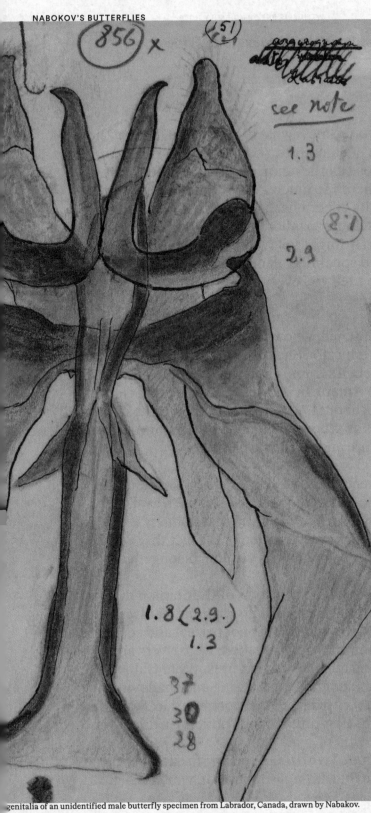

of phantasmagoric state of imagining his specimen being mounted, which is to say being exterminated and then pinned, its wings spread and made ready to view. Boxed, entombed, and put in a little coffin, as it were. That was pleasurable to him, and there's a certain erotics to it. There might also be a certain neurotics to it. As part of that pleasure, which is both aesthetic and scientific, there is the anticipation of the scientific pleasure and an intermediate stage of knowing that this specimen would have to be killed in order to achieve it. It's a very delicate balance, or indelicate balance. The more I read this passage, the more I think it's a confession, not a boast.

151

genitalia of an unidentified male butterfly specimen from Labrador, Canada, drawn by Nabokov.

There's this beautiful couplet from Alexander Pope:

How index-learning turns no student pale,
Yet holds the eel of science by the tail!

It's the idea that if you only know what it is, you don't really know
anything at all. The idea of catching an eel is that it just slithers
out of your hands. You lose all the nuance. Eels are slithery things.
They're rivery things. There's so much to know about the organism,
about its life, and about its experience. The aesthetic level alone
doesn't necessarily contribute to what it is. In the same way, looking at a preserved butterfly might tell you everything that you're
able to ask of a preserved specimen, depending on your classification system, but it doesn't tell you everything you'd want to know
about it in a scientific sense.

EE

I'm reminded of Maria Mitchell, who was an American astronomer,
librarian, naturalist, and educator. She discovered a comet that was
later known as Miss Mitchell's Comet, and she was the first woman
elected as a fellow of the American Academy of Arts and Sciences.
Her story made me think about how astronomy, looking at stars,
and studying the skies is another way of engaging in this overlap
between aesthetic pleasure and scientific pleasure.

ED

There's an analogy between what we've been discussing and the
study of astronomy. Who doesn't look to the sky with awe? Also,
there's art and representation. Keep in mind that in many early
classifications, there was no representation of the fact that a butterfly belonged to a chrysalis, belonged to a cocoon, belonged to a
caterpillar.

Similarly, in astronomy, Galileo, who was of the opinion that the
moon was exposed to various forms of deformation fractures and
fissures and that the celestial spheres were not perfect and complete,
made pictures of the moon showing that there were rivers and
mountains and valleys and all kinds of fractures. What Galileo did,
basically, is what painters do. They use shading and shadows to
invent these realities. The very reality of the moon's surface was being
visually engendered for the first time through optics in a direct way.

EE

Are astronomers also included with those seeking to enforce a meaningful order on a universe that strongly opposes it, which is, I guess,

153

...kov puts a butterfly into an envelope, 1958.

another way of saying putting things into boxes? As a passage of Virgil's from *the Georgics* says, "Labor must be spent on them all, of course, and all have to be set in trenches and tamed at great cost," which is akin to the act of Nabokov gassing the butterfly, killing it, and pinning it down into a box.⑤ The act involved subjugation and suppression. Virgil's words raise a paradox in the practice of farming and agriculture, which involve both violent subjugation and the gentle tending and nurturing of

⑤ *The Georgics* is a poem by Virgil broadly on the topic of agriculture. It is an account of mankind's struggle to order the physical world through farming and husbandry, and the clashes between forces of nature and the desire to establish this order. *The Georgics* was discussed as part of Ed's Fall 2021 GSD course, Histories of Landscape Architecture I, at the GSD in fall 2021. The quote is from the second book of *The Georgics*, line 61–62.

beings. The knowledge that may bring a species or an ecosystem care and benefits may also involve harm or come "at great cost."

ED

This reminds me of Michel Serres, who said that in the Northwest Passage the two most attentive watchers of the sky are sailors and farmers because their lives and livelihood depend on being able to reliably read its signs. These are the people who are mindful of the sky above as they tend either the track of the sea or the furrows of the earth. But then there is the resistance of the earth. It's fruitful. It's bountiful, but it will win in the end. Per Virgil: "Labor omnia vincit." You'll put every last ounce into it. It's arduous. When you work with the earth, as you say, it's painful, it's backbreaking, and it's violent. You cut into the earth and expose it. It's a wound that then is healed. There's nothing pleasant about it because it's not pliant. It has to be worked on.

That's part of Nabokov's story. His first instinct when he wakes up in the morning is to look through those slats at the sky, as if with a scientific instrument. He knows exactly what kind of day it's going to be and how available phenomena are going to be for him to pursue the work he has to do, the work he desires, the work of his desiring.

Nymphalidae: Limenitidinae: Limenitidini

Limenitis arthemis astyanax

(Fabricius, 1775)

60.23

atlanta georgia 7-10 Oct

A sample collected and stored by Nabokov, 1942. Harvard Museum of Comparative Zoology.

⑥ Ed: My mind, as my students learn at their own peril, is very associative, a vast and dusty lumber room of words and images. Much to my regret, I can barely recite even a single line of poetry from memory. Alas, I don't retain words in that way. Now I'm thinking of Shakespeare's (and Sterne's), 'Alas, poor Yorick!' But Emily, in relation to the quote you initially shared from Nabokov, I feel that exact way when I come upon a term and its word or where it fits in. It's almost the feeling of seeing something familiar for the first time. Now I'm thinking of Matthew Arnold's 'so various, so beautiful, so new.' I wish I could memorize Arnold's poem 'Dover Beach.'

EH

You mentioned in prior correspondence that your favorite Nabokov quote is, "Most of the dandelions had changed from suns into moons."

ED

When I came upon that, I was floored. It's one of the most beautiful and compact images I've ever read. The dandelion undergoes this peculiar transformation from a state of a flower to a state of a seed that's going to be disseminated by the wind. Its own viability is at the mercy or the virtue of the winds. They're going to spread it so that it flowers again. Over the course of a day or of a week, the dandelion becomes as full as the sun. It's this corona or aura of light. The origins of metaphor itself is an emanation from the rays of the sun. Nabokov seeing a dandelion, calling it a sun, invokes the role of the sun as a generator of language and the means by which all things are seen and known. Then, in a day, it turns from a solar yellow to an ashen, regolith gray, blown by the air and untethered. The sun is the source of all things that grow, and the moon is absolutely evacuated, devoid of life.

What a gift to see the world in that way. Regarding this line in particular, you can ask my wife, and even my son, who made fun of me because we went on a little walk one day and I said, "There it is. There's the dandelion like the sun," and he's like, "Enough, dad." Language does that to you. I live, live, live in a world of words.© I'm a lepidopterist of images. I want to see them fluttering. I want to pin them down. I want to put them into boxes, everything. I want to see their phylogenesis, their etymology, where they've lived, where they've lost, where they've loved, everything about them.

155

Charlotte Malterre-Barthes is an architect, urban designer, and scholar who was an assistant professor of urban design at the GSD from 2021 to 2022. Her work centers around issues of resource access and related challenges in the urban environment, climate emergency, and material extraction. She maintains an intersectional feminist practice, and is a co-founder of OMNIBUS.

Arnold Arboretum Greenhouses include the Orchard Street and Dana Greenhouses, which were built in 1917, and 1962, respectively. These greenhouses serve the Arboretum by creating a sheltered and climatized environment in which to house non-native plants, such as the Bonsai and Penjing Collections, and to foster new accessions from seed

lotte
erre-
hes
old
etum
nouses

157

→ Raphi Tayvah

RAPHI TAYVAH

On our walk through Harvard's Arnold Arboretum a couple of weeks ago, we touched on so many of our shared interests, including resource extraction and commodification, postcapitalist and climate-vulnerable urban spaces, issues of access, and lost knowledge, to name a few. While I wish we could share the contents of that conversation, I am excited to see where its foundation takes us today.[①]

Thomas E. Marr, *Greenhouses, summer, Orchard Street*, 1919, gelatin silver print.

Let's start with the Orchard Street Greenhouse. This image stood out to me because it illustrates the contrast between the formalized architectural greenhouse structure used to grow specimens for the arboretum and this overgrown vegetable patch in the foreground. As someone whose focus within the landscape architecture field stems from a history

① The original conversation took place on a walk through the Arnold Arboretum and was lost to the fates of technology, but formed the foundation for this second interview.

background, I love this visual juxtaposition and the legible layers that this image offers. It's so charming that this is how the vegetable patch was maintained in an otherwise hyper-curated space.

The Orchard Street Greenhouse was used to grow specimens for the arboretum and process new species acquired as seeds. It played a key role in cultivating newly collected species for the collection.[2] This image demonstrates that there were some productive plants on site. (I am using the term "productive" here to denote a plant's capacity to be edible to humans, which of course has associations with capital value.) This speaks to our last conversation about how the arboretum collection is specifically designed not to have "edible plants" in it.

CHARLOTTE MALTERRE-BARTHES

That's interesting. Someone decided which plants were worthy of joining the arboretum or the greenhouse and which plants were not. What does this reveal about the interests of the time? I am always thinking about the stories that surround objects, especially those that are considered "valuable." There's a whole history behind these plants, not just the history of capital flows or colonial ideologies but also a narration of what was considered to be beautiful versus useful. The movement of plants as commodified goods, which began with colonization, radically transformed the relationships between people and flora. These connections and routes impacted nearly all corners of the globe on a human scale, as well as the classification of plants in relation to each other and their human extractors.[3]

RT

The botanical garden or arboretum acts as a catalog, a living library for landscape architects, horticulturalists, and even the average gardener to come and observe the plants in a natural habitat, providing public access to them. Whenever I visit, the landscape architect in me is drawn to evaluate each specimen for its formal qualities because of the way they are presented, like paintings from my undergraduate art history slides, but I also want to get to know each of their stories.

CMB

The species are taken out of their context, so the narrative of their origins is eliminated. For example, take indigo—a highly

[2] The Arnold Arboretum has a long history of acquiring plants for the collection through expeditions. In its history, a total of 117 such missions have been executed to date. These expeditions resulted in the import of hundreds of thousands of plants and seeds, all of which required processing and cultivation after being removed from their indigenous context.

[3] For more, see Donald A. Rakow and Sharon A. Lee, "Western Botanical Gardens: History and Evolution," *Horticultural Reviews*, vol. 43 (2015): 269–310.

159

commodified plant—into the botanical garden and it becomes just a plant. The role it played in the commodification of cotton, which is at the base of global capitalism today, is suppressed. Without this context, you can claim that it has a certain innocence.

For me, there is something about the botanical garden and this elimination of context that makes it very suspect. The isolation of each species showcases the socially unjust nature of "collecting" for the sake of ownership. The plants do not make the same kind of sense when displayed like paintings as they would in, say, their home forest or meadow. I recall we saw this on our walk a few weeks ago, especially in the vines and shrubs garden. The rows upon rows of specimens all lined up to show off their form felt so out of context with the less manicured trees surrounding them. Since much of my work centers around the flows of material economies and the ways in which they do not exist in isolation from broader history and society, I have a hard time buying into this treatment of the plants.

RT

Do you think there is an analogous conflict between materials and their contexts in architecture or urban planning, disciplines which tend materially to be more static on a temporal scale?

CMB

I'm thinking about the canon. In architecture or in planning, you have a catalog of forms and elements—for example, you're going to need doors, etc.—that are related to more systemic questions like mobility, functions of the everyday, and material systems. The canon, then, is that which dictates a set of given precedents that are "worthy."

For landscape architects, there is also a catalog of potential material that can be used. But the typology of the botanical garden is not considered desirable in landscape. I think the closest thing would be projects like The Jewel in the Singapore airport, which is a futuristic garden, greenhouse, and capitalist destination containing a waterfall and luxuriant vegetation.[4]

One could even think of the botanical garden—not the garden itself but the greenhouse—as the origin of the shopping mall; it is a controlled interior garden environment that is entirely commodified.

[4] The Jewel, which officially opened in 2019, was designed as a collaboration between RSP Architects Planners & Engineers and Peter Walker and Partners. A destination for tourists and locals alike, it was conceived as a new typology of urban park, bringing the park inside rather than the people to the outside.

[5] Paxton's Crystal Palace, constructed for the Great Exhibition of 1851 in London, had an immense influence on the presence of greenhouses in the architectural canon.

This of course arises from the history of the greenhouse as a tool used by colonial empires to control and commodify nature.[6]

RT

Do greenhouses belong to the discipline of architecture or landscape architecture? Or is the greenhouse simply something for the "lower-class gardener"? In this case, I'm referring to the inception of the field of landscape architecture, which was "professionalized" at a time when, in Western societies, the garden was strictly the domain of women and/or field laborers.

CMB

I think that architects definitely **161** claim greenhouses as part of the nomenclature of spaces they can use. But as a singular entity, the greenhouse is something that has moved into industrialized manufacturing. So, there is this idea of cheap luxury associated with the greenhouse. If everyone can have one, then you're speaking about the democratization of luxury. Suddenly everybody can have

...houses, spring, Dana Greenhouses interior, 1962, gelatin silver print.

plants, like orchids, for example. Orchids used to be a very special type of flower that was hard to get because of their growing conditions. Then it became a very affordable, easily accessible type of plant, still completely exotic, but at the same time common. They're a cheap luxury and can be bought at any grocery store here today. And of course, the absolute irony of the orchid is that it's actually a parasite, right? It's something that grows on trees in a very wild way. It's a weed, ultimately. So, it's interesting that it carries this image of exclusivity. It's hyper-commodified as part of a global political economy.

RT

Orchids are such fascinating plants in just about every way. Their formal qualities make them an ideal commodity. They are still "exotic" to Western stylistic sensibilities. It's similar to the bonsai plant, which we also saw at the arboretum. There's a whole industry now around making them into an accessible luxury for the amateur houseplant gardener. They are showing up alongside orchids in grocery store displays, and they can even be bought with those tacky "congratulations" balloons.

Returning to greenhouses for a moment, I'm thinking about how, during the first autumn of the COVID-19 pandemic, every urban restaurant suddenly put up greenhouse-like structures on the street. I love that in order to eat, we were all being put in these small temporary structures similar to those designed for growing edible plants.

CMB

That's true, I forgot about that! The ephemeral but industrial chic of the greenhouse. And it's still prevalent. To go back to the presence of the greenhouse as a typology in between landscape and architecture, it becomes this hybrid space, especially in a home. I'm sure that the one we are looking at in the arboretum leaks. It doesn't matter in that context, maybe it's even a good thing for the plants. But if a greenhouse is also used for housing and living, then it begins to speak to the myth that we live together, humans and that which is nonhuman. We already do this with mold in our bathrooms, but that's not the cohabitation most people want.

RT

Exactly. We all are reliant on fungal species to exist on this planet, and yet we don't want them to be visibly near us in our homes. It's the same thing with so many plants—we need them to survive, but we don't necessarily want them in our backyards. Dandelions are an excellent example, at least in the United States, of a species that was introduced as an edible crop for the lower class and is now seen as an invasive problem. Most people don't even remember that you can eat dandelions!

CMB

I have a friend who is a botanist, and he can cook you up something after just walking through the city. This knowledge has been mostly erased, a fact that has such a colonial–imperial aspect to it, the elimination of knowledge related to self-sufficiency, so people are forced to rely on a controlled source of nutrition. I think one of the most telling examples is that of abortive plants, as we talked about on our walk. We were wondering if there could be a corner of medicinal plants in the arboretum and what that would look like. We don't have that knowledge of "useful" plants, or it's a knowledge that's not accessible to many.

RT

If you could envision a sort of postcolonial arboretum or botanical garden, what would that look like?

CMB

The first thing would be to recognize that there is no innocence in these types of gardens. I think this is something not often addressed. We need to break through the constricted, spatial bounds of the arboretum. But you're asking me a design question, right?

RT

Indeed I am.

CMB

For me, that is a kind of solutionism—how can we fix that? But there are also things that can't be fixed. To start thinking about a more emancipated version of the botanical garden typology, or the arboretum in general, you would need to let it overflow, to find ways of letting it enter the city. For example, by treating all the vegetation in the city as something worthwhile and reflecting on the need to reconnect ourselves to the land that makes it possible for us to live.

163

This rekindling of our relationship with the world around us would have to include a focus on the relationships between knowledge and freedom. Not freedom in the absurd way it's conceived of today but in relation to the fact that you can control what you eat and what you can do to your body via something you find in this arboretum.

RT

Moving to this image of the bonsai kept in the Orchard Street Greenhouse, these "tortured" plants become almost a work of art. They are aestheticized and exoticized so much so that they are no longer called by their common names but rather are named after the craft that shapes them. With this in mind, why is such a high aesthetic value placed on the types of plants that grow in this greenhouse, those that are more ordered or more stylized, versus the types that grow in a wild garden where you could find potentially more "useful" plants? The controlled climate of a greenhouse is a common tool used in agricultural production, so what makes the plants in

an arboretum worthy of using the space as a showcase?

CMB

Looking to the past, I find fascinating instances in which all the open land was transformed into food-bearing gardens. It's this shift from ornamentality to productivity that really shows how separately we think of food gardens in relation to other kinds. I know in Europe, during the Second World War, decorative gardens were suddenly made productive because that was the land available. A good example of this is the transformation of the Bellevueplatz in Zürich into a cultivated field.[©] There is a lot of potential here in turning these spaces into more productive ones, not necessarily by changing the species, but by recognizing that many "decorative" species are consumable.

RT

What is the difference between designing a greenhouse in a more traditional architectural context versus in the context of a productive landscape?

CMB

It would be interesting to think about the greenhouse as a typology with the potential

[©] A case study part of "Plan Wahlen," Switzerland's wartime agricultural policy to ensure agrarian self-sufficiency, 1937–1945. See also: Peter Maurer, Anbauschlacht (Zürich: Chronos, 1985).

: Wolf standing by a bench in one of the Dana Greenhouses, 1966.

to change how we deal with plants. You could create an integrated greenhouse city where interstitial spaces in the urban fabric would become potentially productive via greenhouses. It could include a programmatic component where you grow your own abortive plants and sustenance vegetables. It's also interesting to think about greenhouses as having that liminal aspect. I would be interested in designing greenhouses if they were able to turn the city into a productive landscape that people could use to gain agency.

RT

Greenhouses as a means of social reconstruction. We definitely see this in the discourse around food deserts and off-grid living in the urban context. In cities like New York, there's been a push to inject micro farming as a solution in neighborhoods that are underserved. Of course, community gardens and rooftop greenhouses are a way to break the reliance on the capitalist food supply chain, but it often feels like a neoliberal Band-Aid for a much larger, broken system. How do we as designers shift the function of greenhouses to something truly regenerative?

This leads into my final question for you. When we went on our arboretum walk, I asked you about designing a curriculum centered on a plant. You said you would like to design one around a street tree. Do you think that authoring a syllabus focusing on a greenhouse or even on an arboretum would be a generative project?

CMB

Interesting question. Yes, I remember talking about the street tree in relation to how it would make a curriculum more inclusive of ordinary specimens we encounter on an everyday basis. These trees have so much to teach us about living through extremes. They withstand weather events, road salts, pesticides, noxious chemical compounds, and they share their space with buildings, vehicles, and hardscapes. The greenhouse typology, as we discussed, is potentially something that could foster agency among people. But so is the arboretum, which requires one to think at a completely different scale. I'm not talking about the scale of a site but the scale of the city or even the territory in which you would start to consider incorporating existing plants, such as street trees, into the arboretum. You could turn the whole city into an arboretum! I would think about it as a global arboretum, which I guess defeats the purpose.

Stéphanie Bru and Alexandre Theriot founded their architecture firm, BRUTHER in Paris in 2007. Stéphanie is currently an associate professor at the Universität der Künste in Berlin and Alexandre is an associate professor at ETH Zurich. Together they taught an option studio at the GSD in the Spring 2021 entitled "Borderline(s) investigation #1 – Lightness."

Gropius and Wachsmann's Packaged House was designed by Konrad Wachsmann and Walter Gropius shortly after both architects emigrated to the United States from Germany during World War II. The system, made up of standardized panels, is a prefabricated modular construction intended for a wooden house. Wachsmann and Gropius's research started in 1942 and involved investors and federal funding but failed to become a commercial success.

nie Bru
xandre
riot

s and,
nann's
aged
se

→ Klelia Siska

Konrad Wachsman and Walter Gropius during the assembly of the Packaged House, ca. 1942–1952. Harvard Art Museums.

ALEXANDRE THERIOT

The story of the Packaged House is super interesting. Stéphanie and I didn't know it, we confess!

KLELIA SISKA

It's an interesting case study for an industrialized house using a prefabricated modular system. Kondrad Wachsmann met with Walter Gropius when he emigrated to the United States during World War II, and they teamed up for the design of the Packaged House: a wood house that could be easily assembled from standardized panels using a metal connector.[1] The three-dimensional configurations were endless.

[1] The modular system consisted of 10 types of wood panels, measuring 40 × 120 inches, that could be connected by their edges, at right angles, or side-by-side through Wachsmann's innovation of a wedge-shaped metal node. The panels could be used as walls, floors, or doors, which could be solid or include openings and be assembled into various configurations depending on the needs of the house owner.

Have you ever had the chance to develop such an open-ended model for a project? What was your experience with the building industry?

AT

In our first year as an office, a contractor asked us to develop a flexible, cheap, lightweight construction house model that could adapt to different climates and urban contexts. It was exciting to explore both construction and cost optimization. We chose pure wood construction to explore the structural potentials of the material. This was close to the concept of the Packaged House. Both projects consider how to produce a house cheaply, make a thousand copies, and adapt this process in different regions, different climates, and so on.

These projects are probably too small to influence an industrial product, but making budgetary decisions, beautiful or not, is a lot about solving technical problems.

STÉPHANIE BRU

We need projects of that kind more often, even if they are small-scale. For that reason, it's interesting for us to explore these topics through teaching, which is the best way to activate new thinking for this type of research.

171

KS

I like that you bring up research. I read that when Gropius and Wachsmann developed the Packaged House, Gropius was teaching design studios at the GSD on prefabricated modular houses. So, his students were actually experimenting with prefabrication as a design tool for flexible space configurations. You are both practitioners and teachers. How do you come up with your studio briefs and the research you want to conduct with your students?

AT

I would say we teach what we don't really know. When we were students, teachers came to a university with a body of knowledge. We come with questions instead of knowledge. We don't give an exercise expecting students to find the "right" answer and explain it to them if they don't. Instead, we pose a question that might be impossible to solve. It's a different kind of challenge. For us, the question is just a starting point to explore alternative methods and new possibilities.

In our lectures we talk about bifurcation, a concept developed by the French philosopher Bernard Stiegler.[9] The idea is that there is no single solution to a problem. There are no automatic answers, only opportunities to ask questions. Our approach is less driven by outcomes than by questions. What is the right question to ask considering the site, considering one's preoccupations? I think the question is the starting point of everything.

SB

Works by Lacaton & Vassal and Jean Prouvé's *Maison Tropicale* raise questions about prefabrication and ways of using catalog products in another way. These architects play with the oxymoron of economy and excess. They show that it's possible to do more with less. For us, the Packaged House does the same thing. It's a question of creating space with an economy of means. Its success lies in the different ways of assembling parts.

KS

Exactly. Variability and flexibility were key to the project. In your work, you explore the idea of flexible spaces, but you do this by looking at the elasticity of a given program. You refer to this approach as

② In the book *Bifurcate: There is No Alternative*, Stiegler, along with other editors, proposes the concept of *bifurquer*, French for "to branch off," to suggest ways of rethinking the economy and work in relation to our ecosystem and to reconnect local knowledge and practices with macro-economic circulation. Bernard Stiegler, *Bifurcate: There is No Alternative* (London: Open Humanities Press, 2021).

ls of Packaged House, ca. 1942–1952. Harvard Art Museums.

"uses over program." How did you find yourselves interested in this design approach? Was there a specific reference that sparked this focus?

SB

This interest stems back to our childhoods. Where we grew up, in the suburbs of Paris, children could play anywhere. Cities, by contrast, designate specific places for young people, like playgrounds. This kind of flexibility was our first point of reference. We are always fascinated by informal places, and that led to the question of programmatic transversality. Then we began thinking about the potential of program after seeing the Trevi Fountain in Rome. It's a fountain, but it does more than that.

We have this term in French, *bureau blanc*, or the "white office"...

AT

... it means that you don't have to define anything, you just have a skin or a facade. This was really the starting point for us.

Metal nodes for connecting the panels of the Packaged House, ca. 1942–1952. Harvard Art Museums.

SB

When we started our office, we wondered if it was possible to use this concept to produce a *maison blanche*, or "white house," not because we liked this aspect of architectural space per se, but rather to embrace the concept's pragmatism. What would happen if the walls came down?

AT

One of our first commissions was a 25-unit housing project. The project became a very long and slow process because the client changed the program every six months. Each time, we had to change the structure and the facade, essentially restarting the project. That is when we learned to introduce autonomy between the different elements of the structure and the facade. As Stéphanie just said, we applied the way we think of the flexibility of office spaces to the housing project. The important thing with that project was to be able to change the organization of the apartment. It became a super pragmatic case study on the autonomy of all the building's layers in order to achieve flexibility in its uses, even as the client continued to change his mind.

KS

In the case of the Packaged House, the panels were designed both for walls and floors. So, it could really be reconfigured constantly. There could be no interior walls if needed.

SB

We design with flexibility in mind to win projects. We like to consider how to build without walls. But perhaps it's not just a matter of flexibility . . . but also of preference. We just don't like walls.

AT

Yes, here is our statement: we hate walls! Walls are obstacles.

Flexibility also serves pure capitalistic purposes because this is how the market works. One minute it needs housing, and then the need evolves to something different. That's why all the developers now, at least in France, are so excited about flexible spaces. They see the potential. For them, flexibility is not an architectural question, it's just business. So I think the question of freedom is probably more important than flexibility.

KS

How would you define freedom?

AT

As students we were taught this idea of an architecture in which beauty relies on proportions, such as shadows and so on. This is

175

just pure tradition. More interesting is the question of what freedoms a space can produce. The spaces we design can help us define uses, behaviors, or even pleasures. We try to deconstruct this purpose of aesthetics—the beauty of the space—and focus more on that freedom.

KS

The Packaged House was the product of a specific economy, context, and time: the US during and after World War II. An advanced industry was already in place to develop prefabricated systems used for armament equipment and to house troops. After the war, there was an urgent need for housing, and so many of the existing factories were repurposed to supply the new market of housing construction. Within this context, the intelligent duo of Wachsmann and Gropius joined forces to rethink the new housing needs and developed a design that could be mass-produced, cheap, and easily assembled.

Your built work has also been shaped by the specific context of French suburbs and tight post-recession budgets. But right now you are at a pivotal moment in your practice as you are also getting commissions abroad. How does your design respond to the contexts and industries you are asked to work with?

AT

Jean Nouvel said something like, "You are the pure result of this moment in your culture." We completely agree with that. We are not autonomous. We react to specific conditions of the context, which is the starting point of every commission. Doing projects in new contexts is very exciting for us. Each time it's like restarting our practice, in a way. It requires us to relearn everything and to react to the new, specific conditions. New contexts also mean new economies, so the main question becomes how to manage a project budget. It's always the same story: projects are too expensive. For example, let's say we would like to know what it means to apply this question to the context of the United States. Are there technical answers? Are corrugated steel panels the cheapest, or is it plastic? If it's plastic, what could we do with that material? How do you respond to a new economic context?

KS

Indeed, material choice is one answer. The Packaged House was a wood structure, reflecting the abundance of the material in the United States. Your material choices usually include concrete, steel, and aluminum. Are these aesthetic choices or a reflection of the economy and industry in France?

AT

It reflects the economy. We don't have any specific relationship with concrete, for example. We built in concrete because it was the cheapest way to build in the French market at the time. It was a purely opportunistic decision.

SB

We're not really interested in the aesthetics of a material, we're more concerned with its performance, and that includes its financial performance too. We can work with steel, aluminum, wood, earth—it could be anything. The question is, when does it start to be meaningful, considering a specific context? We are interested in figuring out how to build in another country. Belgium or Switzerland have totally different conditions than France. In the United States, for example, we are fascinated by the balloon frame, which we don't know much about. It's always the same question for us: how will we succeed in choosing the right materials and prefabricated products from catalogs?

KS

Your research has also been focusing on other materials, such as your explorations with fiberglass.[9]

177

AT

Each year we take a material and explore its potential, the limit of its performance capability. Currently we have around six projects that are exploring the potential of plastic. Given the amount of plastic in the world, has it become a natural resource? Why don't we use this material just to build something purely in plastic, not only as a provocation but in regard to the reality of the world's problem of what to do with this material? These are the kinds of questions we try to explore. Our wish is simply to build and to maintain a relationship with the materiality of the world. I mean, architecture is at first a question of gravity and waterproofing. The rest is just decorative elements.

KS

The Packaged House was never actually a successful product. Technology and industry were equally important to the design, so Wachsmann and Gropius set up the General Panel Corporation company to manufacture and sell houses to customers. The company received funding and purchased a former aircraft factory in Burbank, California, for manufacturing, and Wachsmann designed the production layout.[10]

[9] The fiberglass pavilion is a project (or "specimen") led by Theriot as Chair of Architecture and Design at ETH Zurich. It is part of a wider research on glass as a performative material.

Drawing of elevations and sections of the wood panels used in the Packaged House, ca. 1942–1952. Harvard Art Museums.

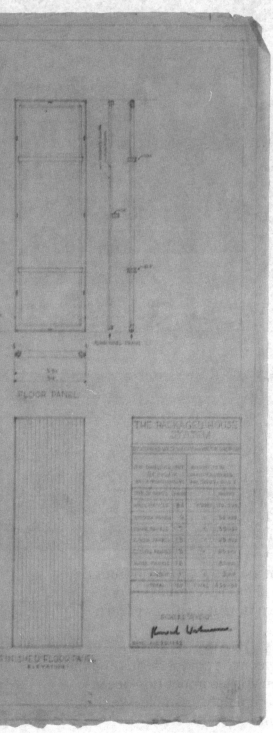

Wachsmann kept changing and perfecting the parts for years. In the meantime, other prefabricated houses came on the market.[5] The momentum was gone. The company closed in 1949. Considering all the energy, budget, and labor spent on the Packaged House, it could be considered a failure.

AT

In an office, success is a necessity because the financial model relies on it. If you enter competitions, you have to win. So does that mean it's a failure if you lose a competition? I don't think that's really the case. Academia and research allow for failure in a way that practice doesn't.

179

[4] As WWII was coming to an end, many of the factories that manufactured armament were repurposed for the housing industry. Federal funds were made available to companies that would take over these factory facilities.

[5] In the book *The Dream of the Factory-Made House: Konrad Wachsmann and Walter Gropius*, Gilbert Herbert follows the complete story of the Packaged House, from its conception in Cambridge, Massachusetts, including the securing of the patent in 1942 and the establishing of the General Panel Corporation, to the the company's bankruptcy. In great detail, the book presents all the funding and stakeholders that took part in the decade-long process of the project, as well as the complicated reasons as to why the project was not a commercial success, such as delays in delivery, Wachsmann's perfectionism, and constant changes to the design. Gilbert Herbert, *The Dream of the Factory-Made House: Konrad Wachsmann and Walter Gropius* (Cambridge: MIT Press, 1984).

Photograph of the General Panel Corporation manufacturing facilities, ca. 1942–1952. Harvard Art Museums.

We take the risk to do something that we know could fail from the start. That's just part of the deal. We should preserve this potential for failure in the process, and learn from it, just as we learn when we lose a competition.

SB

For us, there's no real difference between the competitions and the projects that we build. Sometimes you win a competition because you didn't respect the brief. So, it's completely unstable. We think that possible failure is quite important.

181

KS

And, just as we can learn from failure, crises can also produce some of the best opportunities for innovation ...

The Packaged House certainly pushed the boundaries of architecture and technology, responding to the housing crisis of the time.

AT

As you mentioned, after World War II, the need for housing was so huge that they had to find some answers. There was a shortcut: the fact that an industry was already in place due to the war allowed for an opportunity to produce a massive amount of housing. I think that was a fantastic moment.

People can be lazy. If a business is working, there's no reason to change it. We have to be shaken to change our ways. A crisis will force you to react and come up with new solutions. I'm not suggesting that we need this sort of crisis to innovate. But all kinds of crises, like the 2008 recession, are precious moments. Maybe the war in Ukraine, for example, could be a lever for rethinking energy in Europe. The sudden need to save energy could have quite a huge impact on architecture and the ways in which we address the current housing crisis. I think that is the main question right now.

Production layout of isometric and elevation drawings of the Packaged House, ca. 1942–1952, negative photostat print. Harvard Art Museums.

3

VARIOUS WINDOW PANELS

VARIOUS DOOR PANELS

FLOOR PANELS

CEILING PANELS

PRODUCTION LAYOUT

THE PACKAGED HOUSE SYSTEM
BY KONRAD WACHSMANN & WALTER GROPIUS
1942

Ilze and Heinrich Wolff run the architecture studio Wolff, based in Cape Town, South Africa. Their work focuses on restorative justice and embedded research, and their approach considers the past to act restoratively and imaginatively in the present. Both architects have taught and lectured internationally, including at the GSD in the 2022 studio, "Void infrastructures," and the 2021 lecture, "Homage and Refusal."

Jean Prouvé's "Maison Tropicale" was a prefabricated modular construction system designed in response to housing scarcity after World War II for the French colonies in Africa between 1949 and 1951. All parts were made from folded sheet steel and lightweight aluminum that could be neatly packed into a cargo plane. After many years of existing in Niamey and Brazzaville, the remaining models were dismantled, reassembled, and exhibited in various museums across the global north.

and rich lff x son icale

Kenismael Santiago-Pagán

Jean Prouvé's Maison Tropicale in Brazzaville, Congo. Galerie 54.

KENISMAEL SANTIAGO-PAGÁN

Mireille Ngatsé, of Brazzaville, Congo, was the last resident of Maison Tropicale. Constructed from 1949 to 1952, the house was a prefabricated model construction system designed by French architect and engineer Jean Prouvé in response to housing scarcity after World War II for colonial Africa, specifically Congo and Niger. Ngatsé inherited it from her father, who lived there before her. However, in 2000 the house was dismantled and taken back to France for restoration in exchange for a small amount of money. She later found out the house was being exhibited at the Museum of Modern Art in New York and valued at six million dollars.[①]

How can we begin to deconstruct the postcolonial history of Prouvé's Maison Tropicale to reveal the relationship between Europe and Africa?

① This story is presented by Ângela Ferreira in Manthia Diawara's film *Maison Tropicale. Maison Tropicale*, directed by Manthia Diawara (2008; Lisbon, Portugal: Maumaus).

HEINRICH WOLFF

Jean Prouvé was a great designer, thinker, and French industrialist—at least when he did things in his home country. The moment he started thinking about how to make technical achievements for Africans, things got strange. The main question being, what's the limit of a good idea? It's in the nature of good ideas that they're not just universally good. They're good in a certain place, time, and context. It's one thing to consider how mass production is useful for a population in need of, say, building components, but it's a whole other thing to project a house into a context that doesn't have a housing shortage, such as in Africa. This idea that you mass produce homes, put them on a plane, and fly them over—because Africans supposedly don't know how to build houses—is absolutely absurd. I mean, if they needed houses, they could have just asked the Africans, who know how to build houses for themselves. Why do they need some Frenchmen to fly it across continents?

ILZE WOLFF

Just having this conversation is already a way of thinking through what we can learn from France's colonial conquest. This woman, Mireille Ngatsé, who was the last owner of the house and later discovered its value, I think is the first step to looking beyond Jean Prouvé. Whenever I study these big moments of architectural "excellence," I do question that excellence as a construct, as propaganda. I ask, who are the key protagonists? It's not the Jean Prouvés. It's not France. It's the Mireille Ngatsés.

187

KSP

In what ways did Prouvé adapt his design to take these local factors —people, landscape, materials, economy—into account?

HW

Although Jean Prouvé was precise in designing the ways in which things were assembled, when you look at both models, in Niamey and Brazzaville, you can see that one was built on a flat base and the other on legs. The same legs you see when it's exhibited at the Tate Modern, with the idea being that they allow you to negotiate uneven terrain. Why? Because you're not asking locals how to build on the site. Instead, you make a generic house that is ill-suited, and then you resolve it with steel telescopic legs.

Prouvé's "project" was supposed to be about the efficiency of materials, and flying them across continents is a contradiction of that efficiency. So, his project is not just a technological advancement, it's part of the machinery of colonization, and that casts a dark shadow over his practice. Because colonization is, of course, not just about providing houses for a housing shortage, it is about claiming territory and dominating others through forms of violence.

And this house accommodates that endeavor.

KSP

What are some ways in which we as architects can contribute to decolonizing this territory we've created?

IW

It begins with thinking about modernist colonial constructions and spatial violences that often reoccur because of continued indifference. Indifference toward the architect, toward the author, and toward many experts, in collaboration with Western museums that reconstruct these things. We must deconstruct the propaganda that promotes the old 1940s idea of using design as the solution to complex social problems. How can we then see this as a fable, a story that we can draw wisdom from? Those are the things that we always use in the studio to begin to deconstruct postcolonial moments.

KSP

Deconstructing propaganda makes me think of the institutions where it's generated. I'd like to discuss the argument that the Tate Modern used when they exhibited the house: "To bring Prouvé's Maison Tropicale to London is a historic event, it's a tribute to a great design. And as Britain wrestles with how to go about building the millions of new houses that the government wants, Prouvé's house is a stunning example of how to build new homes quickly, cheaply, and well." Let's keep in mind that people were displaced moments before the house was disassembled, packed, and shipped —first to France, then to Venice, then to London—to be displayed in the 2008 exhibition *Maison Tropicale for Design Museum at Tate Modern*.

HW

This statement by the Tate is revisionist history because it sketches its success only as a technical achievement. That focus tries to eclipse the colonial project and its intentions, as if those aspects are entirely insignificant. That misrepresents its actual history, and it conceals another wicked fact: that this building was stolen from Africa after it was already there. The house was "found" in Brazzaville in 1996, as if it was lying around somewhere in a dilapidated state and riddled with bullets. They don't say it was previously occupied by Mireille Ngatsé, who inherited it from her father, whose family had lived there from the beginning when Jean Prouvé built it. The house was dismantled and returned to France—

IW

—and restored.

HW

Correct. It was as if some mistake had occurred, like a lost suitcase at Heathrow Airport that was found and returned to its rightful owner. Now, this house was sent to Africa inside a container on a plane. This was concurrent with European debates on the masses of stolen cultural artifacts, particularly from that part of the world. Governments were returning artifacts with one hand, while stealing this one back with the other. Stealing the house to return it to France as if we all are in agreement that it belongs there.

KSP

The restored house was purchased by hotelier André Balazs in June 2007, the same year that it was presented at the Venice Biennale. Many scholars think that it needs to go back to where it was first built in Niamey. On the other hand, locals feel concerned that the government won't take care of it. They have a connection to their home but not to the house as a museum object or patrimony, if you will. What does this situation tell us about ownership?

IW

This is one example of a capitalist, industrialist, and colonial ruin. We do a lot of work thinking about the idea of a ruin and how we begin the process of repair. A lot of the time, the repair of the actual

189

CONTAINER N°1   CONTAINER N°2

...iner plans of the Mansion Tropicale kit of parts. Galerie 54.

object is easy. It's a capital injection to repair the building. But then, there is also the repair of the network around that structure, which requires considerably more than capital. It requires an ethical engagement and ethical repair.

For me, to take a building from its context, as if it's an object, is the same as taking a territory. You take a territory from its context, and you make it your own and portray it as if it's an object. That is the condition that European settlers and colonial constructors work around. Everything can be taken. Territories, people, objects, spaces, plants, architecture. So, what is the ethical engagement for us as spatial practitioners when we begin to think about the restoration of these capitalist ruins, these postcolonial ruins? We must understand that these are objects of conquest, of possession, of colonial rule. And, at the same time, they are objects of modernity, which makes them deeply connected to power.

KSP

We are dealing with a housing structure that was deployed across the continent, only to be stolen back years after the experiment failed. Its transformation from a derelict object into a museum object shows the complexity of the situation created by European intervention, which is tricky to unravel in our decolonial moment. People's lives and stories have inevitably become entangled with these foreign-introduced objects. Such that they are both out of place but also impossible to extract?

HW

The house shouldn't have been moved. Its context illustrates its nature, and by changing it, you change its nature beyond what it ever was. I would argue that the adjustments made to the house are highly significant to its architecture because it means that people adjusted the building to be more useful, despite its design short-comings. The house was "found" with bullet holes in 1996 because, if I remember correctly, this coincided with the conflicts between the Republic of the Congo and the DRC.[2] Which makes me remember Jacques Chirac standing with his arm around Mobutu Sese Seko, saying, "What a fantastic friend we have here."[3] The Europeans substantially supported African destabilization. The fact that the house was tarnished with bullet holes is this

[2] The origins of the current violence in the Democratic Republic of the Congo stem from the massive refugee crisis and spillover from the 1994 genocide in Rwanda. After Hutu génocidaires fled to the eastern DRC and formed armed groups, opposing Tutsi and other opportunistic rebel groups arose.

[3] Former president of Zaire (now the Democratic Republic of the Congo) Mobutu Sese Seko Kuku Ngbendu Wa Za Banga was a distinct politician and military officer, who seized power in a 1965 coup and ruled for 32 years before being forced out in a 1997 rebellion.

context. Do those bullet holes have any reference to European presence or actions? If we remove that history, we impoverish our understanding of it, and we manipulate it.

Bernard Tschumi said that the images of Villa Savoye—when it was rotting away and being used as a horse stable—were so fundamental because they displayed an intolerable condition. Villa Savoye could only be modern. It could not degrade. It could not have the patina of time. It could not be a horse stable. It could only be revolutionary avant-garde. In other words, it is not a thing of the future,

Tropicale being delivered in Niamey, Niger, 1950.

it is a thing of the fragile, instant present. These buildings were completed only about 40 years apart, and there's something about the fragility of that proposal that ends up being illustrated by the augmentation of the people's perception of it. This doesn't mean that the architects don't have the right to be radical or propose new things. This is about the story of modern architecture. If we remove European ruins from Africa, we don't have the residue of their degradation to illustrate what really happened.

KSP

The right to be radical must come with an ethical responsibility. Here, we can see the absence of technical achievements. What concerns me is the failure to recognize failure. Not only as an architectural project but as a Newspeak strategy because they wanted to treat a problem that didn't exist in the region with a house that was not needed.④

HW

This image of the plinth in Niamey is an extraordinary image because it shows Jean Prouvé's contribution to Africa: it's nothing. Absence.

IW

Absolutely. Hot empty air. This is the residue of a confluence of many things: post-World War II heroics, false paternalism from the West, the extraction of minerals. So, first we take off the mask, like we've done now. Then, how do we relearn other kinds of emancipatory practices?

Bullet holes were purposely left in the Brazzaville model of Jean Prouvé's Maison Trop after the restoration. Galerie 54.

KSP

Practices of transitional justice as well. That's a really powerful way to engage this topic. To renounce the fundamental proposal in which modernist architects operated, with this genius that arrives with a model and puts it in a table—

④ Coined by George Orwell in 1949's *Nineteen Eighty-Four*, "Newspeak" refers to the ambiguous euphemistic language used chiefly in political propaganda.

IW

—and saves the world with a building!

HW

We can pick on Maison Tropicale, and okay, it's a weak building, but I think there's something important about the world that it existed in. At the time it was designed, Le Corbusier also went to Brazil when he had no work and planned huge buildings to be erected across the landscape as if he had the right to do so. Lots of people went to the colonies and speculated about how these territories could be reorganized, reoccupied, and so on.

Now, there's something allegorical about Prouvé's building. It's not just the idea that it's a design projected onto foreign territories. It's also the building. What happens is that "modernism" perpetuated European styles as the future. And there are long histories of locals just not believing in it. For example, Nehru did not believe Le Corbusier was the right architect for Chandigarh. Corbu brought *modernism* when Nehru wanted *modernization*. It's a different thing. Nehru was clever about where he wanted to take India. Nehru didn't care about modernism, except that it was nonpartisan in a country that was very divided. You can look at many of these buildings that are basically exported ideas projected onto a territory—Maison Tropicale is an allegorical hyperversion. In that sense, we must treasure its history because it helps us to understand the actions of Europeans vividly.

193

IW

For me, this study of Prouvé is useful to begin unlearning some of our habits, but it doesn't yield wisdom on how to practice in emancipatory ways. What, for instance, was being built in and around Niamey and Brazzaville, at the same time, that looked at collective freedoms, communal care, and collective practices, that was not invested in this individualistic white saviorism? Potentially local indigenous architecture or a local modernism that emerged in parallel?

I'm interested in that stuff. Our education is bogged down with these "masters," whether they're good or bad. I'm tired of that. What about the pursuit of collective freedom? I think architecture education should align more with that because, yes, we need to understand the violence, but then we also need to understand the emancipatory practices that emerged despite, within, and because of that violence as well. So that we can actually amplify those practices and build upon them.

HW

We must understand that the celebration of this building today distorts history in an instrumental manner, as a way to sanitize unjustifiable actions. I do think that a building like the Maison Tropicale should be displayed. But there's something repugnant about displaying it without its full history. I think that it certainly should be part of the thinking about modern European architecture and its weaknesses. What is the history of architects, whether they are nationals or immigrants, who lost faith in this idea of the modern project, and then began to reinvent architecture?

You look at lots of settlement-making in Africa, and it was the effort of individuals that was harnessed, rather than that of the state. The strengths of countries like the Congo or Niger go to waste— we lose the opportunity to learn about the ways in which their societies knew how to accommodate their citizens. And I think the concurrency of those histories could begin to give us a better sense of the 20th century, because to talk about modernism is to foreground Europeans. The moment you begin to think across the world, the architecture of the 20th century gets massively diverse. Such additions to architecture narratives will get us to the right place to understand the practices we want to steer away from and illuminate practices that we want to steer toward.

KSP

I find it quite compelling to critique a project while understanding where the profession should be heading. Being from Puerto Rico, raised under modern colonial structures, I ask: Where does the architect stand in relation to this? Where do technical achievements fit into the conversation of oppression and violence? I had a remorseful grudge against the profession. I'm certain there are students like me who are interested in the repercussions of architecture beyond the scale of the building.

IW

We must ask, what kinds of justice can we seek in light of this, and what are the kinds of reparations that we can demand? What are the kinds of repairs that we can contribute to as professionals because let's not forget that we are involved in this as architects? Do we want to be on the wrong side of history? Or do we want to be involved on the ethical side? How do we begin to rescript the disciplinary involvement in this? We must think through these questions as a collective. We can't do this alone. It's not an individualistic pursuit.

HW

I think, Kenismael, that our criticism of a building should not make anyone lose faith in the pleasures of architecture. We love this profession. We love making buildings and having discussions about them. It is irritating to just sit in disagreement with the terms that people are setting. This is not to say that ultimately sociologists or other disciplines will save us, but we need to broaden our understanding of the nature and the consequences of our discipline. We've got to learn from what has happened before in order to do better, but it's not about giving up on it. We certainly love this world.

:y Base, Ângela Ferreira, *Maison Tropicale* (Niamey) #1, 2007.

Marrikka Trotter
is an architectural historian and theorist whose research examines the historical intersections between geology, architecture, agriculture, and landscape in the 18th and 19th centuries. She received her PhD from Harvard University in 2017.

Tanner Fountain
is a fountain designed by landscape architect Peter Walker in 1984 in collaboration with steam artist Joan Brigham. Sited in front of the Harvard University's Science Center. The project is a composition of 159 granite boulders, set in concentric circles, with 32 nozzles that emit recirculated water as mist.

ilkka

tter

ner.

tain

→ Stephanie Rae Lloyd

STEPHANIE RAE LLOYD

Did you know that you're not allowed to take rocks from US National Parks?

MARRIKKA TROTTER

Yes, I did know that! For my birthday last March, I went to Joshua Tree National Park, and it's posted everywhere that you're not allowed to take rocks. Have you ever listened to that podcast, *Criminal*? There's an awesome episode about people who had been taking rocks from one particular national park that was on sacred Native American land.

SRL

I've heard about this! They mailed the rocks back, right?

During dusk in the summer months, the fountain produces a colorful haze. Peter Walker, Tanner Fountain, Harvard University, Cambridge, Massachusetts,, 1985.

MT

That's right. They have this huge collection of rocks that have been mailed back by people who felt guilty or that the rocks have brought them misfortune.

SRL

Have you taken any significant rocks?

MT

I have not taken any sacred rocks; that would be a bridge too far. But I have stolen rocks from national parks. I took a cobble from the cobblestone beach at Acadia National Park, which I love very much and I'm not giving back. I also took a really interesting piece of quartz that had a fairy hole from a different park. You know, like a fairy stone? A rock with a round hole that goes all the way through it. The only reason I know that is because of a high school boyfriend who was into the fantasy genre. In any case, I always felt lucky to have them, not unlucky.

SRL

Good, then you definitely shouldn't give them back.

I'm wondering, did you spend any time at Tanner Fountain while you were studying at Harvard? It was designed in 1984 by landscape architect Peter Walker with artist Joan Brigham. The fountain is composed of 159 granite boulders set in concentric circles, with 32 nozzles that emit recirculated water as mist. It is sited in front of the Harvard University Science Center. Do you remember your first impression of it?

MT

An undergraduate wrote a lovely little essay about Tanner Fountain for *The Harvard Crimson* a while back. I had basically the exact same encounter that this writer describes: didn't register it as being art, and I was a little bit put off by the smell.

SRL

Everyone says that about the smell!

199

MT

Well, when I first encountered it, it smelled a little bit like blackwater that hadn't been completely treated. There was a bit of a sewage-y odor to it. And then, as one does over the course of the osmotic education that takes place alongside one's formal education, I learned about its significance and developed an appreciation for it. But the appreciation was exactly the same kind of appreciation that you might have to develop for, say, Gothic architecture. When you look at a piece of Gothic architecture, such as Harvard's Memorial Hall, as a modern person, it's very difficult to see the building as anything other than a heavy nod to tradition. It's difficult to look at it as a thing in and of itself, with its own properties and its own decisions. You just see a big red brick thing that has a lot of stylistically determined features. I suppose I encountered Tanner Fountain the same way. First of all, you have to understand, I absolutely hate public art.

SRL

Really? Tell me more.

MT

I find public art irritating. It possesses a kind of tortured neutrality because it's gone through so much bureaucracy to strip away any hard edges or controversy before making it into the public realm.

I also find that it comes with a kind of moralizing, schoolmarmy ambition to elevate the "low" taste of the public. My reaction is always kind of like, "Fuck you." I just don't like it. It smacks to me of some weird conservative impulse about raising the tone.

SRL

But isn't your critique of public art having to cede to bureaucratic processes also applicable to architecture?

MT

No, there are a couple important distinctions. One is that built into a piece of architecture is a certain necessity for it existing. There's always a reason why enough people with enough money were persuaded to put their skin in the game and make something where there was nothing. It's not because it has a use that I like architecture and I don't like public art. All that public art has is its appearance in the world, so that's what everybody focuses on.

By virtue of the fact that a building has a use, there is a certain amount of latitude in relation to its appearance in the world. The hardcore consensus-making often happens elsewhere. Also, the bureaucracy that surrounds the successful built project in terms of getting permits, meeting zoning requirements, stuff like

Conversation among the steam produced by Tanner Fountain in the winter months. Peter Walker, Tanner Fountain, Harvard University, Cambr MA, 1985.

that, is nothing like the arbitrariness of public art commissions. With a building, you have minimums that you have to meet. A building in the public realm is like a more traditional landscape in that way. You're free to do the things that all the best pieces of architecture do, which is to satisfy some current need in a hopefully interesting and unexpected way. But, more importantly, buildings that rise to the level of architecture impart the possibility of a better world than the one that generated that need to begin with. It's very difficult for public art to do that.

SRL

I am especially struck by this idea that consensus-making, in architecture at least, happens elsewhere. This is a common idea in science and technology studies.[①] I took a class at the Harvard Kennedy School with Professor Sheila Jasanoff. She has this notion of co-production, which essentially asserts that consensus-building is a simultaneous process through which groups of relative stakeholders form an understanding of the world.[②] I prefer the idea of co-production to other STS theories that designers seem to be obsessed with, such as Bruno Latour's actor–network theory.[③] Architects love to reference Latour in conversations because ANT is all about materiality and nonhuman actors. It's an easy schematic with which to theorize. But your comments about consensus-building highlight the power dynamics at play for the production of architectural objects.

201

MT

Co-production is an interesting concept, especially when it gets bandied about in academic architectural circles. There are lots of things that we know to be true; we know that the rocks forming Tanner Fountain are much older than the configuration in which they're currently placed and the configuration of all the other matter that surrounds them. They are much older than the infrastructure that's required to produce mist or steam. Whether or not they were legitimately sourced from New England farmland, I suppose, is not the point. I mean, they are big bits

① Science and technology studies is an interdisciplinary field that examines the creation, development, and consequences of science and technology in their historical, cultural, and social contexts. For more, see Ulrike Felt, Rayvon Fouché, Clark A. Miller and Laurel Smith-Doerr, *The Handbook of Science and Technology Studies, Fourth Edition* (Cambridge: MIT Press, 2016).

② Co-production refers to the simultaneous processes through which modern societies form their epistemic and normative understandings of the world. For more, see: Sheila Jasanoff, *States of Knowledge: The Co-production of Science and the Social Order* (New York: Routledge, 2004).

③ Actor–network theory is a theoretical and methodological approach in which everything in the social and natural worlds exists in constantly shifting networks of relationships. It posits that nothing exists outside those relationships. For more see: Ulrike Felt, Rayvon Fouché, Clark A. Miller and Laurel Smith-Doerr, *The Handbook of Science and Technology Studies, Fourth Edition* (Cambridge: MIT Press, 2016).

of granite, and as such, they're metamorphic rocks that have a certain duration in their uncut state that goes well beyond what we are easily able to understand as humans. The question is, when is it helpful to keep that in mind, and when is it much more helpful to think about those boulders arranged by Peter Walker and Joan Brigham, in their current configuration, as a new understanding of what that fountain can be? I guess what I'm saying is that an idea like co-production may be a very accurate way of understanding how architecture and all other human endeavors are produced. The question is, is that just a nice thing to know? Or is that useful and powerful when it comes to how we think about our discipline?

SRL

What are the implications of knowing how something is produced?

MT

Maybe the more fundamental question is if there are any implications. John Ruskin put together an incredibly insightful and scientifically accurate understanding of the raw material that goes into any particular piece of architecture. For instance, he talks about the founding of Venice as a geological condition of possibility before getting to the particular features of a particular society at a particular time. And this society was then able to erect the parts of Venice he found most admirable. But, at the end of the day, Ruskin was completely unable to propose any durable or interesting architectural concepts. Now, he had a lot of really valid critiques. But one thing that you realize when you get to be my age is how easy critiques are compared to creative work.

Maybe ideas like actor–network theory or co-production are enough to go on. I think this is kind of how architecture works; these ideas make you excited about something, and then you go off and do some kind of bastardized, inaccurate, fundamentally myopic, and individualized interpretation of these concepts.

SRL

In design, it's easy to fall too deep into these theories and schematics in a way that can be paralyzing. I like that you're describing these concepts as, perhaps, the catalysts to design ideas, but they don't necessarily have to be the be-all end-all of what we produce.

MT

But also, these schematics are not going to tell you what to do as much as you want them to. So here's my helpful hint, which I stole from Jesse Reiser. What produces work? Work produces work.

ther at Tanner Fountain. Peter Walker, Tanner Fountain, Harvard University, Cambridge, Massachusetts, 1985.

When you're like, "I don't know what to do, I don't know what decisions to make, I don't know how to begin this, I don't know how to keep it going, and I don't know how to end it," you have to actually look at other work. You're not going to find that by reading X, Y, or Z, although those things may be helpful and inspiring and all the things we just said. You're only going to find that by looking at other pieces of architectural design with informed eyes. You have to look at them and ask, "What are the decisions that are being made here about envelope, or about aperture, or about the relationship between interior and exterior, or about the relationship between a building and its site?" Very specific things. If you know a couple pieces of architecture that really sing for you, and you say, "I want to work on that project," then you have work that can produce work to start with. The GSD has a history of producing articulate and deeply confused graduates who are able to read and write with the best of all human-kind, but they may not have yet found for themselves any strategies for doing architecture.

SRL

Let's interrogate that phrase "doing architecture" further. Do you mean, "how to produce a built object in the world"?

MT

I mean: "How do you think like an architect in the specific way that only architects know how to think?". That doesn't mean that the only way to do that is to produce built work. There are awesome examples of people who produced almost no built work who ended up having a really significant impact on the field.

Building is a shortcut because the act of building forces you to develop your ideas. Building forces you into a hierarchy of decision making—"I can live with this; I can't live with that; I have to figure this out; I don't have to figure that out"—which simplifies and clarifies your own thinking. It's a shortcut to build some shit because you just kind of have to do it.

When you're just ideating conceptually, nothing forces you to do that beyond the basic act of articulation, which is kind of a false hope because it only involves thinking through language. The idea that just writing something or saying something will clarify a concept in architecture is, I think, a false hope.

There are other ways to develop your architectural thinking to the point that it's significant. That can happen in the publication of images, drawings, models, animations, videos, blogging about things, and on and on. But, honestly, the only way that you know that you've done something significant in architecture is when you see its ramifications in the world. And those ramifications cannot simply be accolades from within academia. That's actually remarkably insignificant, and I say that as an academic.

SRL

How do you know if you've produced something that has ramifications in the world, especially if you are working within an academic context?

MT

Well, I think there are two ways. The first is the most sincere form of flattery. When you see other people taking up your forms and ideas, then you know you're onto something. The second is if you are receiving attention and interest from fields outside of your own. How do we know that Tanner Fountain is an important piece in the "landscape as art" movement? It's not because we know that Peter Walker has become an important landscape architect. It's not because Walker engaged Joan Brigham, who is a pretty important conceptual artist, as a steam consultant. It's not because of what anyone within landscape architecture has written about it. We know it's an important piece of "landscape as art" because an undergraduate writing in *The Harvard Crimson* decided to take it up. That's how we know it matters in the world, because it becomes a thing that draws you in, that makes you interested in looking something up in a field that's not your own. If a piece of architecture is important, I would expect creative minds from other fields would want to talk about it. I would expect that the press would write about it, good or bad. I would expect that you would find that some of the ideas you believe and your project espouses would crop up in other people's work. What is the infection potential? Is it difficult to catch, or is it Omicron-catchable?

SRL

What's the infection rate of an idea?

MT

How does it spread? For instance, with a figure like Frank Lloyd Wright, regardless of how many actors were involved in his work that were not appropriately credited as cocreators, at some point you'd say, "That guy was pretty fucking individual, and he produced an entirely new way of thinking about massing and articulation that remains a valuable source for people today." Same with someone like John Hejduk, who built almost nothing. Hejduk, in his own weird, insular way, was a public intellectual. He was out there doing shit, and he had a community of other creative individuals around him that were interested in what he was doing, and I think he was interested in what they were doing.

205

SRL

We're using lauded white men to make these points. How can emerging designers cultivate the confidence to know that what they're doing is important enough that other people will pay attention?

MT

First of all, I don't think that people who are doing important work always know that they're doing important work. What they have that other people don't is not necessarily even confidence. What they have is way more commitment than ordinary people living ordinary lives of quiet desperation, as the line goes. They're all in. That's true in all fields that I know of.

SRL

So, it is what it is? I also struggle with this idea of "commitment,"
especially when we question the socioeconomic implications
of what it means to be "committed" to the discipline. Who can be
committed and totally all-in? Usually, it's the people who have a
financial safety net or social capital by way of connections within
the industry.

MT

Eh, I know what you mean. But I don't mean "commitment to the
discipline" as some voluntary priesthood that recruits only from
the elite. Architecture has sometimes billed itself that way, as public art has too, by the way, but that's just lame. I mean committed
to *something* that you personally love and feel particularly good at.
You're committing to your own project and to your own success
at that project, and you're willing to go all-in for the same reason
you push all of your chips forward in poker: because your cards are
amazing and you feel like you have a real shot at the entire pot.
And for those who don't ever feel that way about whatever they do
to make income, all I hope is that they feel that way in some part
of their lives. Because that's their real work: that's what they are really committed to, even if their circumstances do not yet allow for
them to make it their full-time pursuit. It doesn't have to be some
elite creative hobby, either. It could be raising their children or tending their garden or YouTubing their craft projects. It's whatever
makes them feel alive and excited.

Now the way we've defined architecture over the past several
hundred years is indeed as an elite white man's pursuit. And yes,
most of the people we are used to referencing as precedents come
from that group. That doesn't mean architecture was like that before the relatively brief period of European historical dominance,
and it doesn't mean it will be like that in the future, even in the
very near future, as that period begins to wane. Historiography
can point to this proleptically.

SRL

How so?

MT

We might be able to recover people who have been treated as mar-
ginal figures and turn them into figures of more significance. There
are lots of people, including myself, who are working on aspects
of that important task. But one thing you can't do is say, "I wish the
past were different. Therefore, I'm going to redefine the boundaries

of the field such that I'm now saying that architecture is 'X' because I say so, and I wish it were." You can't do that because you would end up in the corner of the room talking to yourself. What you can do is say, "I want the future discipline of architecture to be radically more inclusive than the recent past." But the easy way to do that is to give students a steady diet of critiques that point out all the things that are wrong with architecture, including all the ways that architecture is, let's say, racist or misogynist, or has been in the past.

What happens when you do that? I have actually seen this play out. Let's say that you take a recent publication like *Race and Modern*

installation. Peter Walker, Tanner Fountain, Harvard University, Cambridge, Massachusetts, 1985.

Architecture: A Critical History from the Enlightenment to the Present. It's a great book filled with really interesting essays, but it's entirely grounded in critique. Then you start assigning readings because you're like, "I need to cover history somehow, but I don't want to be so white man-focused, so I'm just going to cover history by pointing out all of the ways in which architecture has been implicated in larger systems of injustice, racism, gender discrimination, etc."

The product of that, and it's a logical product if you think about it, is going to be a bunch of disenfranchised, ideologically empowered graduates. Let me explain why this is bad. They're not going to like architecture because they think architecture is at best a guilty pleasure and at worst something that should be addressed by being destroyed or critiqued. If they try to make architecture after that, and all they know is what they don't like, they will have no ground to stand on. There will also be people who are just turned off from architecture, the field in which they just got a graduate degree for which they paid a lot of money.

The other part is what I was saying about ideology. What happens when you have a whole bunch of neophytes who are just hatching

Snow-covered Tanner Fountain. Peter Walker, Tanner Fountain, Harvard University, Cambridge, Massachusetts, 1985.

out into the world, and all they know is, on the one hand, what they don't like, and, on the other hand, that they are right? They have a limited capacity to explore their own worlds with openness, humility, wonder, curiosity, inspiration, ambition, and imagination. Instead, they are bound by an unthinking allegiance to the received opinions of others, like the Catholics were in the Middle Ages. Fucking hardcore. This is not the way that you generate creative solutions or engagements with the world as we know it. We are facing extraordinary shifts and challenges in our time, and I think people feel as though those shifts are catastrophic and preemptive. If I can put it in as utopian a way as possible for rhetorical clarity, the only way that we are ever going to derive joy from our one precious life and create a better future, is to embrace with wonder, curiosity, and interest everything that we are capable of understanding about our worlds as a potential point of engagement and opportunity. In other words, we have to be in a mindset to take risks, to make decisions, to have a creative point of view, and to invest. What does that investment look like? It doesn't look like houseplants, macramé, and a work-life balance. It looks like over-the-top, *I'm passionate about this. I will die trying.*

SRL

I feel like, right now, there's no space to develop personal opinions. You know exactly what your social bubble believes, but there's no time or space for critical reflection or inquisition. I wish we had a buffer zone of time to mull things over, instead of having to synthesize in real time in order to have an immediate and correct reaction. But I guess that's asking a lot of what is ultimately a cultural condition right now.

MT

Well, I do think architecture has a role to play there. What architecture is really good at, and what architects are really good at, is, as Michael Hays would say, "inflecting the cultural imaginary."[4] I think you're absolutely right. Maybe the opposite of wonder and curiosity is judgment, and that's where ideology becomes really damaging. What if we sub out ideology for ethics? Ethics are ways of being and acting in the world that we agree as a society are positive and reasonable and decent. Oftentimes, when we get very judgy, when we react to other people who think differently than ourselves—ethics go out the window. We actually stop being kind and curious because we're so sure that we're right. You're right, it is a larger cultural condition. But that doesn't mean that somehow it's too big for an individual to address. It just means that your work has to be so compelling that it has that infectious quality we were talking about earlier, so that people get out of their default setting.

209

Let's take this back to rocks for five hot seconds. Let's imagine we teleport ourselves to a glacier in the Andes, and our breath is taken away, like that ridiculous painting by Caspar David Friedrich, *Wanderer above the Sea of Fog.* In that moment, our capacity to judge is swamped by a capacity to wonder. Experiences like that, of things that are very alien to us. I think this is why rocks have a special power in our cultural imagination, because we recognize that they're so fucking old. They're also so different from us. They're mineral, and they're

[4]"Re-enchanted architecture: a conversation between K. Michael Hays and Marrikka Trotter," *Architecture at the Edge of Everything Else* (Cambridge: MIT Press, 2010).

complicated, but not in the way that humans are complicated. We see them, and we mark space by them, but they think nothing of us. They think nothing at all. They're remnants of the fact that the planet upon which we live is not stable and, in fact, is constantly moving things around. Ruskin talks about this, about just how ephemeral and insignificant humans are. Rocks are always *memento mori*, reminders of death.

SRL

It's disarming.

MT

Yeah. It's disarming, and it's also freakishly alien. That's a helpful way to think about the power of rocks. The unhelpful way to think about the power of rocks is to try to fetishize them. What's bad is when architects say, "Hey, you know what? Architecture is hard because it's creative work. So I'm just going to borrow some kind of fetish from over there, and I'm going to use it as a form of justification for what I'm going to produce because God forbid I actually have to think creatively and not know what to do."

SRL

It's displacing authority and agency onto an external thing.

MT

It's architects turning their attention to the smaller scale and lower complexity of art without any training in art. Sometimes this includes a lot of appreciation for and knowledge about art, but still relatively little training in art. Rather than trying to do something that might actually qualify as a piece of significant architecture.

SRL

I don't know what to say right now, Marrikka. You're not wrong.

MT

It goes back to what I was saying about critique being easier than creativity. To say, "Hey, I'm cool. I don't like architecture. Let's make a rock." For me, I'm like, "No, actually, I love architecture. Can you do something? Can you help me because I want to rethink the world?"

SRL

In your conversation with Michael Hays in *Architecture at the Edge of Everything Else*, you discuss how being apathetic toward architecture is ultimately unproductive, which feels like maybe we've come full-circle?[6]

[6] Esther Choi and Marrikka Trotter, *Architecture at the Edge of Everything Else* (Cambridge: MIT Press, 2010)

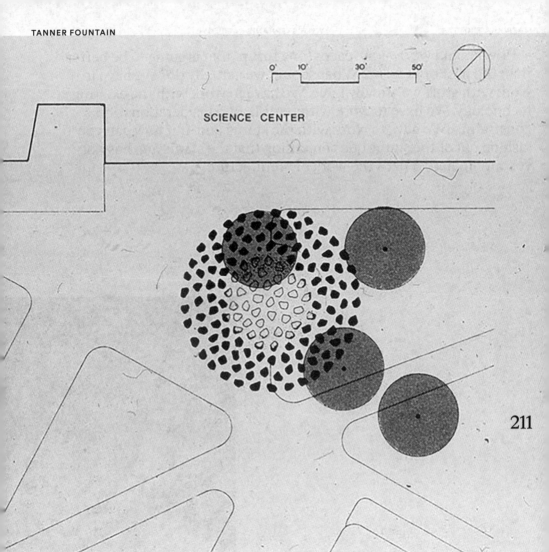

SCIENCE CENTER

211

of the Tanner Fountain. Peter Walker, Tanner Fountain, Harvard University, Cambridge, Massachusetts, 1985.

MT

The one thing that I remember fondly from that conversation with Michael, which might bear on what we're talking about, is what it actually means to do negative architecture.

One way that you might formulate negative architecture is through an architecture of critique. But that's a pretty impoverished stance. Better to deem negative architecture in the sense that it says, and I think I'm paraphrasing Michael when I say this, "Hey, I don't know what the future is going to be, but I can help start describing the space where it might appear." That's an awesome ambition for archi-tecture.

How should we design spaces for a future that is going to be better than the past or present? What should we actually do? We have to work with stuff we already have. We have to work with the existing technology. We have to work with real client considerations and constraints. We have to work with the status quo. But how can you fashion out of the status quo something that the status quo has not yet anticipated? That's the work of architecture.

As editors, we believe investment in one's design work does not preclude engaging in fair and reasonable labor practices. We support pay transparency, particularly by the firms of professors in practice and those who hold administrative positions. At *Pairs*, we have had many conversations about labor and pay, particularly because the annual grant provided by the school in support of this journal cannot be use to compensate student time and work. While we have editorial autonomy, we know this journal is a valuable asset to the GSD, and we hope the continued efforts of *Pairs* teams will keep questions of pay and labor practices afloat as future editors take the helm.

of Tanner Fountain from the Harvard Science Center. Peter Walker, Tanner Fountain, Harvard University, Cambridge, Massachusetts, 1985.

Marianela D'Aprile ⟶ **Universal News Volume 3, Release 7** is a critic and writer based in Brooklyn, New York. She is currently deputy editor of the *New York Review of Architecture* and serves on the board of the Architecture Lobby. Her writing on labor, gender, and culture has been published by *Jacobin, Latina Magazine, the Architect's Newspaper, the Avery Review,* and *Metropolis Magazine,* among others.

is a newsreel released by Universal Studios on January 19, 1931. Such compilations of national and local news clips were shown on a twice-weekly basis at movie theaters from 1929 to 1967. The Universal collection was deeded to the National Archives in 1974.

→ Olivia Howard

"New York, N.Y. – Sky-line for masque ball! Beaux Arts fete features novel architectural costumes," Universal Newsreel, 1931

OLIVIA HOWARD

We're watching a clip of architects dressed up as their skyscrapers at the Beaux Arts Ball in New York in 1931. It is part of a Universal Newsreel from the 1930s, a compilation of short film clips with accompanying headlines, which were presented twice weekly before feature films at movie theaters.[1]

These newsreel stories, deeded to the National Archives in 1974, "featured national and international news and events, politicians, celebrities, performing animals, sporting events, the latest fashions, fads, trends, and other 'oddities.' Local stories might show politicians, parades, football games, beauty contests, or other community activities."[2] News, in other words, that didn't print as well as it *showed*. Does the appearance of corporate architects in building costumes alongside—

MARIANELA D'APRILE

Horse races, train wrecks—

OH

—suggest that their profession was a concern of the general public?

MD

This attempt at entertainment is a bit at odds with the architect's typical self-importance. The clip fails to create any kind of identification with the city at large. It feels like an inside joke. I watched it several times and thought it was pretty uncanny. Creepy, even.

OH

I can see why it strikes a sinister chord. Actually, the first Beaux Arts Ball took place in Paris at the Académie des Beaux-Arts in 1892. The school represented a shift in the architectural discipline when the newly minted "architect" entered into the modern professional world. At that time, the architect was no longer a polymath or a subject of the king but a professional person with services for hire.

The Beaux Arts school brought a European way of thinking about architecture to American education. I wonder if it landed perhaps a little bit differently in the United States given the economic context?

MD

The first thing that I think of is what role the Beaux Arts movement had in the United States in terms of, one, shaping education, and two, defining how people working in architecture in the US in the late 19th century would see themselves vis-à-vis Europe. For example, the World's Columbian Exposition in Chicago was an attempt to show that the US could have as good architectural production as Europe.

My instinct is that there was an interesting underdog mentality that existed in the United States until private interest became more involved in architectural production. And then American architecture started to become about symbolizing corporate prowess rather than civic value. I think, in some ways, the Columbian Expo was still trying to do this.

217

①"One of five major US newsreels, Universal Newsreel was released in theaters from 1929 to 1967. It consisted of edited stories released twice weekly as issues arranged in annual 'volumes,' averaging ten minutes per issue initially and six or seven minutes in later years, with each newsreel containing several stories." Scope & Content entry, National Archives Collection UN: MCA/Universal Pictures Collection, 1929–1967. Series: Motion Picture Releases of the Universal Newsreel Library, 1929–1967.

② James Konicek, "A Moving Image 'Newspaper': Universal Newsreels at the National Archives," *The Unwritten Record* (National Archives and Records Administration's blog, Special Media Records Division), December 30, 2013.

OH

Each of the architects in the clip corresponds to a skyscraper built for some of the biggest corporations at the time: William Van Alen, architect of the Chrysler Building; D.E. Waid, the New York Metropolitan Life Insurance Company Tower;

Steward Walker, the Fuller Building; Leonard Schultze, the Waldorf; E.J. Kahn, the Squibb Building; Ralph Walker, One Wall Street (the Irving Trust Company Bank Building); and J.H. Freedlander, the Museum of the City of New York.

Each represented capital in a way no building ever had before. As you wrote in your *Avery Review* article "Notes on Tafuri, Militancy, and Unionization," "architecture sought to escape its academic and Beaux Arts orientations and realign itself to support the development of industrial capitalism."[3] I thought that was very concisely put.

MD

When we talk about American architecture, even to this day, there is an implicit comparison to Europe, in terms of buildings that exist in the public realm because they are primarily commissioned by or sponsored by private capital as opposed to public interests. And of course, this is going to result in very different aesthetics. That is very pronounced in what modernism becomes in the US, compared to what it was aspiring to be in Europe.

Mies is such an interesting example because he was willing to build for anyone, which I think is kind of emblematic of architects. He built a monument to Rosa Luxemburg, but meanwhile was the architect of a lot of incredibly pro-capital architecture in the United States. I think that that's really emblematic of not only that switch between public and private interests, but also of the way that architects have had to capitulate to whatever and whoever is in power in order to get their work built. Architecture is incredibly labor- and capital-intensive, and if you don't have labor and capital, you can't make it at all. It's not like being a painter or a sculptor.

OH

The practice requires architects to remain allied to capital.

MD

The alliance of power to those able to marshal labor capital is always there—everywhere—no matter what. That predates the Industrial Revolution, and it will outlive our globalized neoliberal present.

OH

The Beaux Arts Ball, as a tradition, is institutionalized through architecture schools, which usually host their own parties every year, often with the same name. Here in New York the Architectural League puts one on each year. In my eyes, it seems like architects use it to claim their status in the professional class, in the same way that doctors and lawyers have their own galas. Is the

[3] Marianela D'Aprile and Douglas Spencer, "Notes on Tafuri, Militancy, and Unionization," *Avery Review 56* (April 2022)

ball a tool to socially reify the architect as a professional rather than, to quote Adolf Loos, as a "bricklayer who knows Latin"?

MD

Or as a laborer or—

OH

—a craftsman, a draftsman, exactly.

MD

Well, what are parties for, in general? Parties are for solidifying someone's belonging to a certain group, right? Your friend has a birthday party. You're invited. You are in that group. You're not invited, and you're out of that group.

Also, to me, the costume aspect is really interesting because it's not like you have to wear a black tie! I'm obsessed with architects' obsession with outfits. It's so important, right? I was working at an architecture office and I would wear outfits that I liked, but they weren't workwear. And someone was like, "You're going to work in that? What?" I had to explain to them, "Well, it's more important to show that you have your own style than to wear business casual or comply with whatever office dress code." People are judged based on what they wear. There's an expectation that in order to be stylish you have to have your own style; you have to give yourself an identity. The way you dress yourself is interpreted as your ability to design as an architect.

219

OH

Design yourself, basically.

MD

Yeah, you craft yourself to be a billboard for your work. And in some ways, it makes sense to me that someone who is interested in design and aesthetics would be equally interested in their outfit as they are in the plan for a building that they're designing. To me, it also feels just as plausible that someone would not care at all about fashion, because all of their creative energy is going toward the building that they're designing. But that's often unacceptable in this world that we're referring to. You are as much on sale and on display as your work is.

OH

Right. There's a huge identification between your *person* and your *work*. Do you think that reinforces the idea of the architect's individual work and individual intellect? Compared with all of the invisible and disregarded labor that actually goes into building a building—

MD

100 percent.

OH

—that is not dressed up in cool glasses and chunky rings—

MD

I think the way in which it gets reinforced in graduate school is really unhealthy because you are taught that you need to build out a niche for yourself and that you are really selling yourself as a particularly good thinker or designer or both. I think there's equal emphasis on both your *work* and your *self*. Those things start to become conflated.

What happens in many cases is that people end up having really tortured relationships with their "work" once they enter the labor force. Often they're designing for a principal, and technically all of their labor belongs to that person and is going to have that person's name on it. Their authorship goes completely unnoticed. But because they have also been taught that what matters is their individual contribution, they're kind of unable to understand what is happening when their labor is being alienated from them through the process of working for someone else.

There's this cult that says, "Actually, it's your work that's really important." And maybe you're doing a stint in a firm right now— five, 10 years, however long— but eventually, you're going to be able to do your own thing, open your own office, and finally put your own name on the drawings. I think having that as the ultimate goal and aspiration can often keep people from understanding

INFORMATION SH

KINOGRAMS NEWSRE

120 West 41st Street, New York City

Sent by ____CHARLES MACK.____
Subject ____William Van Al- Ny Sky line.____
Place ____N.Y.C.____   Date____

IMPORTANT!!   Ship your film with one copy of this sheet in but NOT in the can. For fast delivery ship parcel post special deliv Chicago, Cleveland, N. Y. State & New England States to Kinog Grand Central Terminal P. O. Box 277, N. Y. City.   All other Kinograms Newsreel, General Post Office Box 301, N. Y. Cit COPY OF THIS SHEET WITH NEWSPAPER CLI EDITOR KINOGRAMS, 120 W. 41st St. DO NOT MAI TO THE POST OFFICE BOXES.   Send negative undevelop PANCHROMATIC FILM MUST BE PLAINI

1. Long shot of William Van Alen, Architect of Chrysler Bu:
2. Close up of J.E.Waid -- N.Y.Metropolitian Build.
3. Steward walker
3. Group shot of ...S.Walker,Fuller Build,Leonard Shultze.He L.J.Lahn,Squibb build.W.Van len,Chrysler Build.Ralph W D.E.Waid,New Letropolitan Life,J.H.Freelander,Museum of
4. Closer pan of same.
5. L.J.Lahn Squibb building.
6. J.H.Freedlander Luseum City og N.Y.
7. Miss L.Cowan wash basin,...J.Arwin boiler
8. Close up of Van len,Chrysler Build.

This is all that could be obtained.Every body in a terr hurry.

WHO ELSE COVERED?
none   Total Foo

"Information Sheet Kinograms Newsreel" listing content to be included in the Universal Newsreel and 250 feet of total footage.

what is happening to the products of their labor when they're doing it collectively and "anonymously" in an office setting.

OH

Your point about alienation from work is really interesting, because for those who resist labor politics in architecture, that is the essence of labor extraction (which Marx wrote about). At the same time—maybe it starts at university—you're taught to compete rather than to collaborate and create the best possible project together. It's about your individual portfolio, your individual achievements . . . .

MD

This model of education that is built around the contribution of the individual is a Beaux Arts model.

OH

How so?

MD

Well, in the Beaux Arts education model there's a small crew, and students work under a master. Each student is competing to come up with the best design to then hopefully be an apprentice under the master.

OH

Sounds so contemporary. It's like people who get hired out of their studio reviews.

221

MD

Yes, exactly. That still happens. But the scale is much larger, right? Maybe in the late 19th century, in Paris, one or maybe two schools were like that. And now there are, like, four studios of the same size at one university out of however many . . . . How many professional architecture programs are there in this country? More than 100?

I remember in my first-year Architecture 101 class the professor announced, "only about 20 of you are going to be professional architects."

OH

Classic.

MD

Right! I remember thinking, "Then why are we all being taught as though everyone will eventually open their own firm?" Because those are the skills that you're given. Everything that is related to the way an office actually works is taught in courses that are given way less weight and importance than studio. Or you have to learn on the job. I think that makes the first, like, 15 years—if we're counting education as part of your career—really hard. Really difficult.

You leave school ill-equipped for the labor force or with a surplus of skills in one area and a deficit in another. You leave school by the time you're 24 or 25, and oh my God, that's still so young—your brain isn't done forming!

OH

Your frontal lobes are—

MD

—almost cooked but not quite. And you have been fed an understanding of how your working life is going to be that is just incongruous with reality. It's no wonder that it's taken this long for architects to start looking at their labor differently. I think it's happening now because the conditions under which people are working have just gotten so terrible. And the dream of going to work at OMA and then starting your own firm is remote. People have done it, but we

"Miami, FLA. – 80 to 1 shot wins sensational race at Hialeah Opening," Universal Newsreel, 1931;
"Coney Island, N.Y. – Dangerous Steps mark new figures by daring skaters," Universal Newsreel, 1931.

are really seeing how rare that actually is. And the reward of doing that is ever smaller. We can talk about it in Marx's terms: over time, the rate of profit falls. It makes sense that the profit that you could have stood to make from your job as a sole owner of an architecture firm 25 years ago was way higher than you could today.

In the United States, people's lives have gotten materially much more difficult in the last few years, even looking back over the last 40 years. People are more aware that there is no hack or shortcut. People are starting to say, "Okay, well, it's not realistic that I might open my own firm, even if I go work at OMA, because I have student debt, because my rent is really high. I can't afford to pay someone. Even if I could afford to open my own firm—"

OH

"It would just be me."

MD

"—and I would be drowning in work." So it's like, "Okay, that's off the table. Realistically, until I retire, if that ever happens, I can only work... I'll always be working at a firm." Then the question becomes, "Okay, well, how do I make that better?"

OH

Well, there are mechanisms to keep you at a firm, like promotions. The corporate structure is an incentive to stay with the company.

MD

Yes. Ladder climbing. In some architectural contexts, that's actually quite difficult, because you'll see firms that have maybe two principals and then 15 associates and that's it. I think it's in those contexts that people are looking around and realizing, "Okay guys, we've all been here for a while. We're all probably going to be here for a

den, N.J. Undersea to the North Pole! Sir Hubert Wilkins inspects "sub" in preparation for perilous voyage." Universal Newsreel, 1931; York, N.Y. – Sky-line for masque ball! Beaux Arts fete features novel architectural costumes," Universal Newsreel, 1931.

223

while. What's up? What can we do to make this better? We all need pieces. We know our boss makes half a million dollars a year and is on vacation right now. Let's get a piece of that." I think that's why we're starting to see people, architecture workers at different offices, starting to try to unionize.

OH

It was a really exciting moment when the SHoP workers announced that they had voted to unionize. That resonated for all of us. Even though it didn't go through, do you think it's still a success on their part? For me, it clearly communicated solidarity not just among working architects but also outside of architecture. It was the first proper acknowledgement of class in the architectural workplace. And we don't talk about class in the United States. Ever.

MD

It's true. It was a huge success. I think any time workers organize, it's something that should be celebrated. Just because they didn't win their first campaign doesn't mean that they can't do another one and win.

OH

And especially at a time when Amazon, Starbucks—

MD

—Apple! I think it's emblematic of the times that we're in.

OH

You're affiliated with the Architecture Lobby, too, right?

MD

Yes, I'm on the board right now. I've been in the Lobby since 2015. I have another year left on my term.

OH

What has your experience there been like?

MD

When the Lobby was founded in 2013, it was much smaller. And then eventually it became a much larger organization with membership and chapters. I think for a while what it did was give people a way to meet other like-minded architects. And I think even just that is a huge task.

But I think it's also had other really huge successes. For example, in 2017, we ran a campaign called #NotOurWall. Do you remember the southern border wall request for proposals?

OH

Yes, all kinds of firms submitted actual proposals. It was shocking to see.

MD

We did this campaign that asked architectural firms to sign a pledge saying that they wouldn't submit. But realistically, there were only three firms in the United States that could have taken on the work because it was a massive project that required architecture, engineering, and construction. And through organizing, the Lobby actually helped to get one of those three firms to rescind the proposal that they had already submitted.

OH

Wow! I didn't know that.

MD

It had a real impact, but it also gave a lot of people their first experience organizing their coworkers, the experience of talking to a colleague and saying, "Hey, I think that our firm should sign this. What do you think?" And sometimes those conversations are really hard to have, and it was, I think, a big success that the Lobby was able to identify an issue that people cared about and that people were going to mobilize around.

Since then, there have been other really great projects. But probably the biggest success is making labor and architecture something that people talk about, which I think no one really did before. And I think even just that is huge.

OH

What we're learning now, in graduate school, pertaining to professional practice, is, "How can I enable myself to practice in this economy?" It's more about the architect-developer, author-owner structure, where entrepreneurial innovation can happen.

In researching the Sherman Act, I learned that this was the first moment when architecture had real stakes in big development.[4] I'm thinking, for example, of John Portman's project. He was also a developer. Does that have any bearing on the future of organized labor?

MD

Yes, but first it becomes a question of understanding what is actually at stake when we talk about architecture. The value of architecture comes from land values, and how much money a developer is willing to put into a building comes from a calculation of how much money they think they will be able to get out of that building as, most often, rental property. So in my mind, this question needs to come along with another question: "What are we fighting for in our workplaces?"

For example, in New York, there is a local law that just passed, Local Law 97, that reduces the city's carbon footprint by 40 percent by 2030 and by 80 percent by 2050.[5] But it actually needs to be implemented.

OH

Reduce emissions through building code.

MD

Yes, and through building retrofitting. That's an area where organized labor in the building trades, engineering, construction, and architecture could really place pressure on city officials and even on their bosses to make sure that buildings

225

[4] The Sherman Antitrust Act was enacted in 1890. It was intended to limit monopolies, price-fixing, and other restraints on competition in the free market. Though professions such as law, medicine, engineering, and architecture were initially exempt from antitrust laws, injunctions against the American Institute of Architects in 1972 and 1990 curtailed the possibility for architects to collectively coordinate for better pay. See Peggy Deamer, "The Sherman Antitrust Act and the Profession of Architecture," *Avery Review 36* (January 2019)

are compliant and Local Law 97 is actually being implemented correctly. That's a different thing than workplace conditions.

Are we also fighting for better quality buildings? A lot of developer-driven buildings are crap because they use really horrible materials. In the developer's interest, they want to keep the cost per square foot as low as possible and then charge as much as possible per square foot for rent so that they yield the highest profit possible. And then there's also just the simple fact that developers are given so much legal leeway. They're basically in complete control of the public realm. And what little control the "public" still has over the built environment is being sold away to more developers.

OH

Maybe the fact that New York both has a strong sense of public life and an intensely capital- and developer-driven real estate market—

"Hollywood, Cal. – Dance stars lead dog's life! Dumpsie and Waffles in hectic rehearsal for big revue," Universal Newsreel, 1931; "Readville, Mass. – 50 injured as trains collide at crossing in blinding blizzard," Universal Newsreel, 1931.

and a skyline constantly under construction—makes organizing the architectural labor force there more possible in the first place?

MD

I try to correlate these things to the scale of the problem: working conditions are the smallest scale, and the fact that developers have enormous amounts of power is maybe the biggest. Ultimately, I think all of those things can be addressed through the power of organized labor. The size of the problem is obviously also commensurate with the amount of labor power that you would need to have in order to actually fight back, right? In order to get better working conditions, you just need to organize your coworkers. In order to fight the power of the real estate lobby, you would need to organize

⑥"Local Law 97 is one of the most ambitious plans for reducing emissions in the nation. Local Law 97 was included in the Climate Mobilization Act, passed by the City Council in April 2019 as part of the Mayor's New York City Green New Deal."

every single worker in the city and probably some politicians too.

OH

That's a useful way to think about it. In a similar vein, it seems to me that the design-build model is responding to this dynamic with the developer that gives architects very limited means within which to practice. But there is also no inherent tool or filter that is going to prevent an architect-owner from behaving in the way that a developer does, because development isn't . . . a personality type, it's a protocol, right?

MD

Yes. And as soon as you become a developer, your material relationship to the building that you are making changes—even if you're also the architect—because now your interest is to make as much money as possible. That's not a moral judgment, it's just your interest.

227

and, Cal. – Rush to Complete Marine Models for 1932 World's Fair," Universal Newsreel, 1931;
York, N.Y. – Dempsey gives Baer technical knockout victory over Heeney," Universal Newsreel, 1931.

If you want to have a business model that's viable, you're going to want to make as much money for your new building as possible. It can't be helped.

OH

It's beyond good and bad, yeah. What about cooperatively owned businesses? Is that something you see as a viable solution to the kind of problems we're talking through?

MD

I think they are a solution to the problem of fairly dividing profit. But the reason that solution is less important than, let's say, unionized workplaces, is that for me, the ultimate goal is always increasing the power of workers across the board.

To use an example, one of the big problems in architecture is that there aren't enough women or people of color. What happens is that a lot of the time, they will start at an architecture program and then drop out because they typically make less money or they have less generational wealth, and architecture can be a very expensive education. The rate of attrition is such that by the time people go through school and get their first job and everything else, the statistics of women and people of color in the field are terrible. Something like 8 percent of architects are people of color and about 30 percent are women.

OH

Are you serious? At the university it's still pretty equal because women tend to be really good students, intelligent (obviously), and really hard working. Is it the workplace dynamic that filters?

MD

This filtering is not at the educational or disciplinary level. These are societal-level problems.

Let's say you have women and men graduating architecture programs at the same rate. But then they enter the workplace, and it bottoms out. Why? Because the working conditions are probably very long hours, and women are still primary caretakers in a lot of situations in their homes, and then they're expected to work 80 hours a week? That's not going to cut it. Or maybe they're facing sexism in their work. Or they're being compensated 77 cents to the dollar, and that's not enough money.

I think the only way to fix these labor issues is through a strong labor movement that can put pressure on people, whether it's bosses or whether it's the government directly. For example, do we want more people of color to see through their education? The only solution to that, in my opinion, is to have free public education, including at the tertiary (college) level. The only way that we're going to win that is through a very strong labor movement that can fight for it.

OH

It's ironic looking at the way SHoP reacted to the unionization effort despite their being so famous for their cooperative model and progressive values. Their response was so abrupt and hostile and also alluded to how a union went against their progressive values.

MD

A co-op model is not going to fix those things, even in the workplace, because a co-op model can't fight for a contract that says we're going to have wage parity. So, I don't think it's a bad model, but it doesn't address the real problem. If we're looking at how we are going to try to fight for change not only across the profession and the discipline but also across society and all of the things that feed into the profession, then we have to talk about how to organize labor.

OH

At the beginning of my architecture education, I was drawn to academia because it was a place where you could be critical. There was space to think about things, read, and reflect. But I'm not sure if that's still a real pursuit, actually, once you get to professional school. How do you see your role, as a journalist, maybe, or a critic, outside of the binary between practice and the academy? A third thing is sorely needed.

MD

I'm just a writer, and I work also as an editor. I'm not a journalist. I do criticism. To give some background, I have a BArch from the University of Tennessee and practiced in offices for a very brief period of time. But I was always more interested in architecture as a subject rather than something I would make. I went to grad school for history and theory at Berkeley.

I've always been interested in architecture because I thought that it was a really capacious vessel for understanding how the world works. It is an expression of so many things, in particular, who has power and how much and how they express it. And I always thought 229 that it was a really good lens through which to understand the world. So, my writing tries to do that, to use architecture as a way to elucidate bigger things about the world that we live in. I might be more or less successful at different times with it, but that's always my goal.

I think the binary between architecture and the academy or practice and the academy exists because they are completely different professional worlds. That makes sense to me. But I think the complaint going from practice to the academy is that academics live in la-la land and have no idea what it actually takes to make a building and are divorced from the reality of construction.

OH

Because they don't have to contend—

MD

Yes, they don't have to deal with practical problems. And the criticism from the academy about practice is that there's not enough thinking outside of the box and people forget historical context and things like that. Often, the reason this dynamic is continually fed is that these two audiences are just talking to each other. However, I think people who work in architecture, no matter what they do, are actually in constant conversations with the public, just through the fact that buildings are engaged by a lot of different people. That's also how I think about my work: addressing the general public as much as possible and understanding that whatever I'm writing affects a broader audience than just architects.

OH

I really appreciate that you brought up the "audience." Let's fold it back into the original object we discussed, the clip of the 1931 Beaux Arts Ball. The producers at Universal Pictures would have had an average or mass American consumer in mind when distributing this newsreel. Architecture is a mass medium too.

MD

Yeah, 100 percent.

OH

And I wonder what your perspective is on how it speaks to the public these days. When I was a younger student, I loved reading for the first time Neil Levine's *The Book and the Building*.[6] The ambition of architecture to communicate to the public—even as directly as print or screen media does today—registered instantly for me. But beyond the melodrama of "ceci tuera cela," do you think architecture still speaks to people?[7]

MD

Yes, of course it does. And right now, most of the time what it's saying to people is "Fuck you." And it sucks, but that's also the world that we live in. Or actually, most institutions are saying to most people, "Fuck you."

And I think that the way that we can say "Fuck you" back is by organizing.

[6] Neil Levine, *The Book and the Building: Hugo's Theory of Architecture and Labrouste's Bibliothèque Ste-Geneviève* (1982).
[7] Victor Hugo, et al., *Notre-Dame de Paris* (Paris: E. Renduel, 1835).

Katarina Burin ⌒————→ **Freud's Dream House** ⌒
is an artist whose work is influenced   is a house designed in 1931 for Sigmund
by modernism, architecture, archives,   Freud's daughter. It was destroyed
historical documentation, and femi-   by Nazis during construction and never
nism. In addition to her own artistic   completed. Architectural drawings
practice, Burin is a lecturer on visual   of the house were included in
and environmental studies at Harvard   *The Interpretation of Drawings: Freud
University and was a 2017 Radcliffe   & the Visual Origins of Psychoanalysis*,
Fellow.   a 2021 online exhibition with Harvard's
   Museums of Science and Culture.

rina
rin
id's
am
se

Adrea Piazza

ADREA PIAZZA

The object we are discussing today is a drawing of Freud's "Dream House." There is very little information about this house and very little documentation. What we do know is that it was designed in 1931 by Felix Augenfeld and Karl Hoffman for Sigmund Freud's daughter Anna and her partner Dorothy Burlingham, who were both talented psychoanalysts in their own right. During its construction, the house was destroyed by Nazis and never completed.

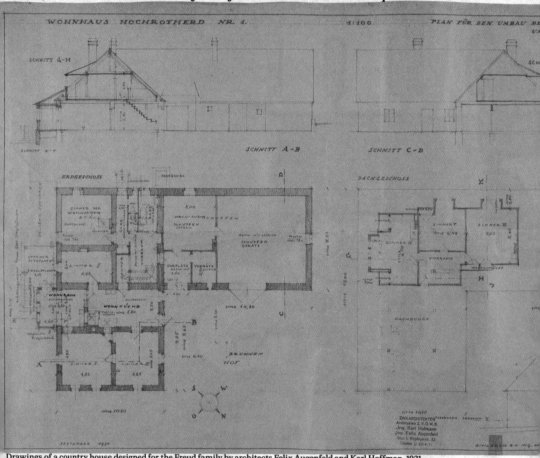

Drawings of a country house designed for the Freud family by architects Felix Augenfeld and Karl Hoffman, 1931.

KATARINA BURIN

It sounds like a perfect fiction. While I was studying at Yale, I took a Freud's Vienna class, and I became obsessed with the Vienna of the turn of the century. That Freud existed in this climate is not surprising; one gets the impression that this time period was particularly prone to the fiction of the Freudian male genius and the hysterical woman. Repression was so embedded in the culture there at this time.

AP

Repression, of course, was one of Freud's obsessions. The online exhibition where we found the drawing of the "Dream House" attributes this in part to his fascination with censorship, which he witnessed at the border of Russia and in postal communications with his sons during the First World War.[1] Freud began to fixate on the idea of what was missing, what remained unknown. This anxiety bled into his spatial mappings of the mind, which include unconscious or repressed areas.

KB

It's one thing to think about censorship conceptually. But think about people whose job it was to open letters, actually, physically, and then read through them and decide what needed to be censored. Like a love affair, for instance. That is fascinating to me.

AP

Me too. Freud was interested in this very active censorship—people literally scratching out information.[2] In the case of history books about architecture, censorship is represented by a more passive absence; information isn't physically scratched out, rather it's not put on the page at all. The canon we study fails to account for various absences. You take up this failure in your own work by addressing one particular absence, that of a woman architect in the modernist era. How did this topic come to interest you?

235

KB

When we lived in Slovakia, my mother was a civil engineer. She studied architecture and practiced in a firm in Bratislava when I was a young child. Moving to Canada thwarted her career. She would have had to take new licensing tests, and she was still learning English, so she got a job doing AutoCAD drawings where my dad worked, a company that made radar detectors. We had a fairly traditional, patriarchal family structure, so my mother was the primary caretaker. I have often felt uneasy about the fact that she didn't fully

[1] *The Interpretation of Drawings: Freud and the Visual Origins of Psychoanalysis*, Harvard's Museums of Science and Culture, 2021.
[2] Censorship techniques at the Russian border included "caviar" (blotting out passages with smears of black ink) and "paper overlay" (pasting paper directly onto the page to conceal text or images).

get to practice what she planned to, but she never spoke about this with me, so I may be projecting.

But this does make me think about how there are so many different points in which someone's career desires could be thwarted. There are countless missed opportunities, unheard voices, people who don't get where they want to in life. We never learn about them. In my work I've been trying to talk about that in some intelligent way, to quantify it, to eliminate speculation, or rather to highlight speculation.

AP

Petra Andrejovna-Molnár, or P.A., who I should mention is the fictive modernist architect whose body of work you created, is indeed based completely on speculation. In your project, since P.A. never existed, you are inventing access to her as you further develop the story. You are rendering visible an absence by producing her presence. It's subversive in a way. The more you build up this individual and discover her work, the more specific her body of work gets, the more detailed, the more comprehensive, and the more it calls upon the vastness of what we don't know. It pushes against itself in a way that I find so beautiful.

Freud does the same thing in his own drawings and diagrams of the mind. The mind is an invisible, unknowable entity that Freud brings into being in a spatial, physical way. Within the diagram of the mind, he represents the repressed bit. The mere act of representing it as such brings it into being. In describing its unknowability, he makes it known.

KB

It's fascinating to try and render the unknown visible. The very thing that you cannot actually visualize, or express in words, or apply any logic to is the driving force behind the decisions you make. The subconscious that you're dealing with—that repressed thing— is the part that you don't see and cannot access. And that is precisely the thing that's really forming your personality. I guess it does speak to my project. I hadn't thought of that.

Making drawings of architecture, the house, the "dream house" —all of that kind of makes sense to me. The drawings use a familiar language so we can better understand them as spaces. But drawing the mind makes me think about my frustration with finding ways to talk about this thwarting. It is this huge invisible thing that you can't really grasp; there's no way to track what happened when and why.

AP

Or what didn't happen.

KB

What didn't happen, what could happen, what almost happened.
. .

AP

I've had the book *Contribution and Collaboration: The Work of Petra Andrejova-Molnár and Her Contemporaries*, the culmination of your longer project, on my desk in Gund Hall for the past few days. A handful of people have passed by and sort of paged through it. No one has questioned her existence. It's completely plausible that P.A. is real, especially when you are introduced to her through the format of a printed book. The form of the object certainly facilitates the plausibility.

KB

When I started the P.A. project, all I wanted to do was make a book of this fictional person's work and put it out in libraries and on bookshelves, never claiming that she wasn't real. I'm still a little frustrated that there is a reveal in

237

ese sketches, Freud experiments with how to represent a topographic model of the
he. A later iteration of this diagram was published in his 1932 volume *New Introductory*
res on Psychoanalysis.

the text, at the end of the book, stating that it's my project. At first, I didn't really want anyone to know that it was a fiction. That's why, in exhibitions of her work, I included the work of her contemporaries. It seemed more believable to embed her into a canon.

AP

I love the introduction, written by historian and Professor of Architecture Sean Keller. He raises this idea of architects inventing names for themselves ("Le Corbusier" and "van der Rohe"), wearing costumes ("the cape, the glasses, the cigar"), and manipulating images ("doctored photographs, pasted-up collages"). There is a theatricality, a mythic quality to architecture that is highlighted in your work.

KB

Yes, that's a beautiful text. Often within the story of architecture, you don't know what's real and what's not. There's a lot of performance involved. It's an imaginative, fictive world to a certain extent. And that's just an inherent part of any architecture project. Plus, it is weird that in the case of so many architects, one person gets the credit when there is a huge team behind them.

AP

Your project feels a bit like a critique of the singular genius.

KB

Exactly. I talk about collective practice a lot, even though I'm trying to give P.A. some authorship. I do try to embed her work into that of her peers—all these men who are making things in Vienna between the two wars. It was this incredibly fertile moment between the two wars and the rise of communism. Everything that was built and dreamed up was very utopian and idealistic. It was all about reducing that stately, singular wealth of the large villa in favor of living together and providing housing to people who didn't have access to it.

AP

You redrew real drawings by P.A.'s contemporaries to include in the exhibitions. Why was it important to you to remake them yourself?

KB

Well, I was fascinated by this moment in modernist architecture. I knew it would be impossible to get access to the real drawings for my own exhibitions, and I was also curious about the fact that I was so in love with them. It was fetishistic. I'm always questioning what this obsession means to me, and I'm very aware of how it could be problematic. Why do I love the things I love? If I remade a drawing, would it feel as authentic? Would it have the aura of the original? I had to make several versions of the drawings. Sometimes things would go wrong because I was trying to do everything the way they did it, with pen and ink. And then, eventually, I would produce one that had the feeling of the original for me, and that is what I would use in the exhibitions.

AP

In looking at P.A.'s work, I'm really interested in the literal process of creation and replication. But beyond the physical process of drawing, I wonder about the emotional process of creating her work. How much of yourself was a part of that? Did you have to consciously relinquish your sense of self and embody her, or did that just happen naturally?

KB

It's a really good question. I was trying very hard to embody this other person, to not see myself in my work. I think part of the impetus of this project involved not knowing the exact nature of what I wanted to say personally. Architecture drawings became this wonderful escape because there's a poetics to them, but their goal is to be functional. I really loved embodying that coolness and dryness because I had always felt that I was this sentimental, emotional person in my work. I used to make drawings that were full of aura and nostalgia. I was overly focused on the past and my childhood in Slovakia, and I hated that. I wanted to destroy that.

239

AP

Can you talk more about your childhood?

KB

I was six when my family left Slovakia, but from my early days of making art and drawings, I was always looking at communist architecture as a model. I don't fully understand what that means to me or what it meant to me at the time. There was this fascination with concrete, with these decrepit surfaces, and with an obviously false facade of things going well, not knowing what's happening underneath. Because I was forced to move away from it and because it was cut off from my life, I had this desire and longing to understand it and to make it and remake it. This architecture is very much a part of my memories of how we lived in those six years.

That's something I've been trying to understand: why am I always going to the past? Maybe it's about archives and storytelling or about the potential to retell a story. I do think that now I'd like to live more in the present.

AP

I'm struck by your urge to reject the idea of aura and nostalgia in your work given that you are still so fascinated by your childhood. How do you understand that conflict?

KB

Well, sometimes "nostalgia" implies believing that the past was better than it really was. I felt embarrassed about looking at communism as this thing that I longed for. I was trying to understand it through the disparate bits of information that I had, such as photos from my family archives of us hanging out in certain places and some weird, fuzzy memories. In a way it relates to Freud, envisioning the aspects of my childhood that I can't see.

I think if I had stayed there, I would have a very different relationship with it. I would have seen it changing and would have grown with it. But when you leave a place and you're not allowed to go back, you just want access to it again. And of course, in my memory, I had a fairly happy childhood, and my parents sheltered us from their difficult experiences witnessing communism and not wanting to be part of it.

AP

You were just six years old.

KB

Yes, and at that age, I loved all of the communal activity that I remember experiencing on vacations by the sea or on simple camping trips with friends and family. It felt different from this singular-American-nuclear-family-in-the-suburbs kind of thing. I think my initial wariness of the past had to do with not understanding what it was that I was nostalgic about. Now, with distance, I can be

Burin's 2016 drawing of Petra Andrejovna-Molnár's monogram design from more curious and selective about what it is that interests me about that past, and I can look at it critically.

AP

You mentioned that you didn't know the nature of what you wanted to say personally, which is what led you to pursue this project. As an artist, how did you work through this?

KB

There is something about inventing stories and taking on different personalities that has been a running theme in my life. Perhaps this makes up for the feeling of not knowing exactly what my contribution to the world should or could be. But I often find a kind of secret way of figuring it out, like creating work through a different voice or a semi-fictional character. Some people have a very clear agenda for what they want to communicate and they go for it. I've just never felt that.

That also stems from my culture a little bit. I was raised by modest, Eastern European Catholics. My parents constantly said, "I couldn't possibly do that" or "I'm not good at that," and I felt this sense of self-negation growing up. Entering the world of North America and witnessing the confidence that people present themselves with was quite enlightening.

241

So there's a lot going on there. It's funny that you ask that question because I haven't really thought about it so much, but this project was an access point for me. It gave me so much agency because I could just pretend. I could pretend to be competent and able, like an architect.

AP

By embodying another character, you can do anything you want.

KB

And it always was about her. It wasn't as though I was making these time-consuming, anachronistic architectural drawings by hand for myself, right? Because they were for her it was okay, you know what I mean? She made them.

AP

It sounds like inhabiting her persona helped you find your own voice.

KB

It did! You asked whether I was personifying P.A. or if I was myself. In the end, I would look through the work of P.A. and think, "God, it still looks like my work somehow." I was trying to mimic other styles and channel other voices and even have other people draw for me, yet the work still had a specific aesthetic. I couldn't escape it. I just wanted to make something that didn't look like I made it.

AP

In a way, isn't that reassuring?

KB

Yes! There is a voice.

That said, I hated the project while I was making it because it was more than just designing and drawing P.A.'s work. It was also about the captions, the wall text and exhibition design, and everything else. At shows, curators would sit down with me and say, "Let's go through these captions, because I'm getting different dates for the same drawing." And I would just mix it up, I was confused by those details. The curators would say, "Look, I'm a trained art historian. I cannot have misinformation in these captions." And I would say, "I know, I'm sorry, but it's all misinformation!"

AP

You are certainly an unreliable narrator in the telling of P.A.'s story. But I trust your unreality (the fictional character P.A.) more than the reality we are presented with (the absence of women like P.A.). You know? Your version must be more real than the version in which there were no women designing things.

KB

What I love about history and archives is that we often take for granted things as real and as actually having happened. But then you think, wait, did it really happen like this? I'd been studying the work of Charlotte Perriand, Eileen Gray, and Lily Reich and look-ing at all these players in this modernist world. They were very independent and lived unconventional lives. I romanticized their lives and how much they were able to achieve. But I was frustrated with the fact that I kept coming up against these few women. And I thought, there must be more.

AP

In your life as a person or an artist, do you think about being a woman? Is that a part of your thought process?

KB

Yes, especially when I was doing this project. In the normative world that I inhabited growing up, I felt oppressed by my gender. I had thoughts like, *I can't do certain things. I'm not smart enough. I'm too emotional. I'm too sensitive.*

AP

You, your mother, and P.A. are all operating within similar con-

243

with her brother and mother in their garden plot on the edge of Bratislava, ca. 1979–1980.

straints, despite each of your distinct conditions, real or invented. Often it's only in retrospect that we think, "Wow, I wonder how that impacted me."

KB

I know. It's often subtle things that shape you, that frame your sense of self. That's part of why I couldn't take myself seriously as an artist for so long. I was never able to say, "Yes, I'm serious, I do this work seriously." I have so much respect for some of my female friends who are doing well with their careers and are like, "I have the right to do this, there's no smiling about it. It's not cute. I'm a serious artist."

AP

Of course we should also question how characteristics like that fall along gender lines.

KB

Absolutely. It's years of a certain kind of thinking that we're unpacking. Generations.

AP

Your work seems to identify the space between what's real and not real, recorded and unrecorded. It makes me think of the "third space," a concept you've discussed in reference to your 2019 exhibition, "a low storey between two others," with artist Farhad Mirza. What is this in-between space that doesn't exist? It's like the places that you visit over and over in dreams. They become familiar, spatial, and concrete, but they're not real. They only exist in the space of dreams. I have a few of these places, and I don't know what they are or where they come from.

KB

I was thinking about those dream spaces this morning! There are maybe three or four that I can locate and actually envision that I've been to repeatedly. But it raises the question, have I been there repeatedly? Or, is it that in my dream I thought the space was repeated, and therefore I think it's repeated in real life? I can't tell if it's actually recurring.

AP

The fact that you don't know is the most fascinating part about it. It's as though we're the most unreliable interpreters of our own dreams. Historians, scholars, and archivists, who document architectural history, are unreliable narrators, too. I'm thinking again of Freud, for whom the mind holds a completely inaccessible area. Repressed, scratched out, censored. Through projects like yours we can start to uncover what has been buried, invent what never existed, and construct all the various "dream houses" that were never built.

SANATORIUM

Burin's 2015 replica of a drawing by the Czech architect Jan Víšek depicting Víšek's Silhan Sanatorium, ca. 1929–1935.

Subjects and Objects

7 *Ila Bêka and Louise Lemoine* are filmmakers, educators, and publishers exploring contemporary urbanism through lived experience, trading conventional architectural representations for deeply personal visual descriptions. They currently teach in the Diploma Programme at the Architectural Association in London and gave their first public lecture at the GSD in 2013.

Building Gund Hall is a 16mm film chronicling the construction of the new home for the GSD from October 1969 to August 1972. Designed by Australian architect John Andews, 2022 marks the building's 50th anniversary. The film, directed by Len Gittleman, is part documentary, part art film, part drama, with shots alternating between comedic (and at times poetic) time lapses with messy, on-the-ground close-ups of tradesmen screwing, nailing, and jamming parts together.

21 *Kevin Young* is the Andrew W. Mellon Director of the Smithsonian's National Museum of African American History and Culture and the *New Yorker*'s poetry editor. While a student at Harvard University, he was a member of the Dark Room Collective, a community of African American writers. Young is the author of fifteen books of poetry and prose and the editor of nine volumes of poetry.

Aalto's Woodberry Poetry Room is a special collections room designed in 1949 by Finnish architect Alvar Aalto and housed within Lamont Library. The Poetry Room is home to an unparalleled collection of 20th and 21st century English-language poetry books and serials, audio recordings, and rare materials. It reopened in 2006 following a contested renovation.

33 *Mindy Seu* is a New York-based designer whose work reimagines the history of the internet and public engagement with digital archives. Seu is a graduate of the MDes program at the GSD, where she received the Design Studies Thesis Prize for her *Cyberfeminism Catalog*. An updated manuscript is set to be published by Inventory Press in 2022.

Metahaven, "Inhabitant" was a lecture given online at the GSD about notions of sensing and inhabiting in filmmaking, art, and design. It was delivered by Daniel van der Velden of the Dutch design practice Metahaven in October 2020.

51 *Christopher C.M. Lee* is the Arthur Rotch Design Critic in the Department of Architecture at the GSD. He is the cofounder and principal of Serie Architects in London, Mumbai, and Beijing and has served as the Design Advocate for the Mayor of London since 2017. His work is underpinned by the renewed relevance of typological reasoning and experimentation to describe, conceptualize, and project an idea of the city.

The Smithsons' Golden Lane was a 1953 urban housing competition proposal for the city of London. Featuring a series of 16-story-tall slab buildings linked by a network of "streets in the sky," the proposal focused on four distinct scales: the house, the street, the district, and the city. Although never built, the Golden Lane anticipated the Smithsons' Robin Hood Gardens and challenged post-war housing typologies in England.

67   **Thomas Demand** is a German sculptor working between Berlin and Los Angeles whose work is exhibited worldwide. His one-to-one scale paper models, which he photographs in his studio, often reference familiar images circulated through mass media. He currently teaches at the Hochschule für bildende Künste Hamburg in Germany.

Blaschka Glass Flowers is a collection of plant models crafted meticulously out of colored blown glass by the Bohemian glassworkers Leopold and Rudolf Blaschka in Dresden, Germany, between 1890 and 1936. Originally commissioned by the Harvard Botanical Museum as a teaching collection, today they are on public display at the Harvard Museum of Natural History.

83   **Matthew Au and Mira Henry** run the Los Angeles-based architectural design studio Current Interests. Matthew and Mira are both design faculty at Southern California Institute of Architecture (SCI-Arc) and have taught at Princeton University and the GSD.

Petra Blaisse's Gold Curtain is a space-dividing curtain designed in 2012 by Blaisse's studio Inside Outside for Piper Auditorium in the GSD's Gund Hall. The double-faced curtain serves as the backdrop for many public events and provides flexible spaces for uses at different scales within the large auditorium.

101   **Keller Easterling** is an American architect, urbanist, writer, and is the Enid Storm Dwyer Professor and Director of the Master of Environmental Design program at the Yale School of Architecture. Her writing covers global infrastructures, economies, and policies that shape space. Her recent books include *Medium Design: Knowing How To Work on the World* (Verso, 2021) and *Extrastatecraft: The Power of Infrastructure Space* (Verso, 2014).

Levittowns are considered by many experts the formula for postwar housing strategies throughout the continental United States during the 1950's and 1960's. William Levitt was an American real estate developer who envisioned these mass-produced suburbs in New York, New Jersey, Pennsylvania, and Puerto Rico, creating an unprecedented template that shaped the aesthetics and politics of postwar suburban life in the country.

115   **Mack Scogin and Merrill Elam** are the co-founders of their eponymous, Atlanta-based architecture studio. Active in the professional and pedagogical fields, they frequently teach—often independently, sometimes together, and sometimes alongside architect and filmmaker **Helen Han**. Their voices uniquely complement and contrast one another in multimedia studio courses, such as those they have jointly taught at the GSD.

(nostalgia) is 1971 short film by Hollis Frampton in which he burns a series of photographs on a hot plate. As each rapidly immolates, a narrator describes the content for the subsequent image, pointing to the highly contextual relationship of sound and vision. This film is part one of the Hapax Logomena series and Parts I-VII are included in the Harvard Film Archive.

"Favorite Things" is a series of diptychs assembled from Merrill Elam and Mack Scogin's personal travel photography that often accompany lectures as an unaddressed backdrop. The juxtapositions prompt viewers to reflect on the unexpected similarities that emerge between the renowned with the seemingly mundane.

133   **Alfredo Thiermann** is an architect and co-founder of the firm Thiermann Cruz Arquitectos in Santiago de Chile. He is an assistant professor at the École polytechnique fédérale in Lausanne, Switzerland, and was a design critic at the GSD. His research centers on architecture's generative engagement with other disciplines, namely sound and film.

The Carpenter Center Ramp is a pedestrian ramp serving as the organizational axis of the Carpenter Center for Visual Arts. At its entrance from Harvard Yard, the ramp expresses the original Le Corbusier design, but its termination on Prescott Street is the product of several collaborations over time. It is the only building designed by Le Corbusier in North America.

145   **Edward Eigen** is a senior lecturer on the history of landscape and architecture at the GSD. His research and teaching focuses on the relationship between humanistic and scholarly traditions of the natural sciences and the allied practices of knowledge production in the long 19th century European and Anglo- American contexts.

Nabokov's Butterflies is a collection of materials from Vladmir Nabokov's research on butterflies including during his time as a Research Fellow in the Harvard University Comparative Zoology department between 1942 and 1948. Nabokov's obsessive passion for butterflies is on display in the documents, notes, sketches, and preserved specimens that remain today.

157   **Charlotte Malterre-Barthes** is an architect, urban designer, and scholar who was an assistant professor of urban design at the GSD from 2021 to 2022. Her work centers around issues of resource access and related challenges in the urban environment, climate emergency, and material extraction. She maintains an intersectional feminist practice, and is a co-founder of OMNIMUS.

The Arnold Arboretum Greenhouses, include the Orchard Street and Dana Greenhouses, which were built in 1917, and 1962, respectively. These greenhouses serve the Arboretum by creating a sheltered and climatized environment in which to house non-native plants, such as the Bonsai and Penjing Collections, and to foster new accessions from seed.

69   **Stéphanie Bru and Alexandre Theriot** founded their architecture firm, BRUTHER in Paris in 2007. Stéphanie is currently an associate professor at the Universität der Künste in Berlin and Alexandre is an associate professor at ETH Zurich. Together they taught an option studio at the GSD in the Spring 2021 entitled "Borderline(s) investigation #1 – Lightness."

The Packaged House was designed by Konrad Wachsmann and Walter Gropius shortly after both architects emigrated to the United States from Germany during World War II. The system, made up of standardized panels, is a prefabricated modular construction intended for a wooden house. Wachsmann and Gropius's research started in 1942 and involved investors and federal funding but failed to become a commercial success.

85   **Ilze and Heinrich Wolff** run the architecture studio Wolff, based in Cape Town, South Africa. Their work focuses on restorative justice and embedded research, and their approach considers the past to act restoratively and imaginatively in the present. Both architects have taught and lectured internationally, including at the GSD in the 2022 studio, "Void infrastructures," and the 2021 lecture, "Homage and Refusal."

Jean Prouve's "Maison Tropicale" was a prefabricated modular construction system designed in response to housing scarcity after World War II for the French colonies in Africa between 1949 and 1951. All parts were made from folded sheet steel and lightweight aluminum that could be neatly packed into a cargo plane. After many years of existing in Niamey and Brazzaville, the remaining models were dismantled, re-assembled, and exhibited in various museums across the global north.

197 **Marrikka Trotter** is an architectural historian and theorist whose research examines the historical intersections between geology, architecture, agriculture, and landscape in the 18th and 19th centuries. She received her PhD from Harvard University in 2017.

215 **Marianela D'Aprile** is a critic and writer based in Brooklyn, New York. She is currently deputy editor of the *New York Review of Architecture* and serves on the board of the Architecture Lobby. Her writing on labor, gender, and culture has been published by *Jacobin*, *Latina Magazine*, *the Architect's Newspaper*, *the Avery Review*, the *Metropolis Magazine*, among others.

233 **Katarina Burin** is an artist whose work is influenced by modernism, architecture, archives, historical documentation, and feminism. In addition to her own artistic practice, Burin is a lecturer on visual and environmental studies at Harvard University and was a 2017 Radcliffe Fellow.

Tanner Fountain is a fountain designed by landscape architect Peter Walker in 1984 in collaboration with steam artist Joan Brigham. Sited in front of the Harvard University's Science Center. The project is a composition of 159 granite boulders, set in concentric circles, with 32 nozzles that emit recirculated

Universal News Volume 3, Release 7 is a news reel released by Universal Studios on January 19, 1931. Such compilations of national and local news clips were shown on a twice-weekly basis at movie theaters from 1929 to 1967. The Universal collection was deeded to the National Archives in 1974.

Freud's "Dream House" is a house designed in 1931 for Sigmund Freud's daughter. It was destroyed by Nazis during construction and never completed. Architectural drawings of the house were included in *The Interpretation of Drawings: Freud & the Visual Origins of Psychoanalysis*, a 2021 online exhibition with Harvard's Museums of Science and Culture.

Editors, Contributors, Designer

EDITORS

Olivia Howard is a 2022 graduate of the GSD Master in Architecture I program and holds an undergraduate degree in architecture from Taubman College at the University of Michigan. She is from Dresden, Germany.

Adrea Piazza is a fourth-year GSD Master in Architecture I student and holds an undergraduate degree in English from Georgetown University. She is from Blue Hill, Maine.

Kyle Winston is a 2022 graduate of the GSD Master in Architecture I program and holds an undergraduate degree in architecture from the College of Design, Architecture, Art, and Planning at the University of Cincinnati. He is from Delaware, Ohio.

CONTRIBUTORS

Elif Erez is a 2022 graduate of the GSD Master in Architecture I and the Master in Design Studies program in History and Philosophy of Design and Media and holds an undergraduate degree in architecture from Yale University. She is from Istanbul, Turkey.

Emily Hsee is a third-year GSD Master in Architecture I student and holds an undergraduate degree in architecture from Yale University. She is from Chicago, Illinois.

Linda Just is a 2020 graduate of the GSD Master in Design Studies program in Critical Conservation and received her Master of Architecture from the University of Illinois Chicago. She is from Herrin, Illinois.

Stephanie Rae Lloyd is a 2022 graduate of the GSD Master in Architecture I program and holds an undergraduate degree in architecture from the College of Environmental Design at the University of California, Berkeley. She is from Fremont, California.

Andrea Sandell is a fourth-year GSD Master in Architecture I student and holds an undergraduate and graduate degree from Boston College, where he studied philosophy. He is from Tirano, Italy.

Kenismael Santiago-Págan is a 2022 graduate of the GSD Master in Design Studies program in Critical Conversation and received his Master in Architecture from the Universidad de Puerto Rico. He is from Bayamón, Puerto Rico.

Klelia Siska is a 2022 graduate of the GSD Master in Architecture II program and received her undergraduate diploma in architecture and engineering from the University of Patras. She is from Preveza, Greece.

Julia Spackman is a third-year GSD Master in Architecture I student and holds an undergraduate degree in architecture from the College of Environmental Design at the University of California, Berkeley. She is from Los Angeles, California.

Raphi Tayvah is a third-year GSD Master in Landscape Architecture student and holds an undergraduate degree from Smith College, where they studied art history and museums and translation studies. They are from New York City and Portland, Oregon.

DESIGNER

Team Mao develops creative direction and visual narratives for institutions, brands, and individuals. Based in Berlin, Team Mao collaborates internationally, with work ranging from publications, exhibitions, branding, and campaign design to independent projects and design education. The team Mao design approach focuses on exploring visual aesthetics in a social context.

Image Credits

Ila Bêka and Louise Lemoine

8–12, 14–19: *Building Gund Hall* (1972), Len Gittleman. Property of Harvard University.

Kevin Young

24–25, 28: Courtesy of the Woodberry Poetry Room. Photographs of Woodberry Poetry Room. Collection of visual material relating to the Woodberry Poetry Room, MS Am 3147, Box 1. Houghton Library.

Mindy Seu

36, 39–41, 45–47: Courtesy of Metahaven.

Christopher C.M. Lee

53–54, 60–61: Courtesy of The Alison and Peter Smithson Archive, DES-2003-0001-009455761. Frances Loeb Library.

56: Cluster Diagram, The Golden Lane becomes fully fledged as districts of city. 1952. 37.2 x 23.7 cm. Inv.: AM1993-1-710. Photo: Jean-Claude Planchet / G Meguerditchian. Digital Image © CNAC/MNAM, Dist. RMN-Grand Palais / Art Resource, NY.

59: Golden Lane housing project competition, London: Photomontage with Gérard Philippe, 1952. Photograph with india ink, 44.5 x 64.2 cm. AM1993-1-698. Photo: Jean-Claude Planchet / G. Meguerditchian. Digital Image © CNAC/MNAM, Dist. RMN-Grand Palais / Art Resource, NY.

62–63: Large ensemble of Golden Lane, London Deck. Perspective Photomontage with Marilyn Monroe, Joe DiMaggio, Peter Ustinov, etc. AM1993-1-697. Photo: Jean-Claude Planchet/ G. Meguerditchian. Digital Image © CNAC/MNAM, Dist. RMN-Grand Palais / Art Resource, NY.

Thomas Demand

68, 71–73, 77, 80–81: The Archives of Rudolf and Leopold Blaschka and the Ware Collection of Blaschka Glass Models of Plants, 1886-2020. ecb00006. Archives of the Economic Botany Herbarium of Oakes Ames, Harvard University. Courtesy of the Archives of the Economic Botany Herbarium of Oakes Ames, Harvard University.

Matthew Au and Mira Henry

84: Courtesy of and photograph by Anita Kan.

86, 88–89, 91, 97: Courtesy of Inside Outside.

93: Courtesy of Diandra Rendrajaja. Photograph by Anita Kan.

94–95: Family Dinner, photograph by Shikun Zhu.

Keller Easterling

103: Xmas tree in a livingroom, Levittown, N.Y. 1962., Harvard Art Museums/Fogg Museum, National Endowment for the Arts Grant, © The Estate of Diane Arbus, LLC, Photo © President and Fellows of Harvard College, P1972.7.

105: Curved Streets, Aerial view; Levittown, Nassau County, N.Y. 1949, Levittown Public Library. 1949, Levittown History Collection, Courtesy of Joan Galante, Reference Librarian.

107: Courtesy of Bettmann Archives. The Archive was purchased in 1995 by Corbis, a photo agency owned by Bill Gates, and later sold to VCG which partners with Getty Images for preservation and distribution.

108–109: Images property of Willingboro Public Library, Willingboro Township, New Jersey.

112: Surviving the Floods in Levittown Puerto Rico, Toa Baja, P.R. 2017. Vicente Sanabria and Elizabeth Serrano survived the floods together at a house in Levittown with other neighbors. Courtesy of Photographer Denis M. Rivera Pichardo for the Washington Post.

Merrill Elam, Mack Scogin, and Helen Han

118, 123, 127, 130: "Favorite Things" images courtesy of Mack Scogin and Merrill Elam.

119, 122, 126, 131: (*nostalgia*) images reproduced with permission of the Hollis Frampton Estate.

Alfredo Thiermann

134, 137, 142–143: Courtesy of Fondation Le Corbusier.

136: Exterior view up ramp, Carpenter Center for the Visual Arts. Harvard University, Cambridge, Massachusetts, United States. Courtesy of the Frances Loeb Library Harvard Graduate School of Design (103118); © Olivier Radford.

141: Courtesy of Michel Denancé.